Invisible Listeners

Invisible Listeners

Lyric Intimacy

in Herbert,

Whitman,

and Ashbery

Helen Vendler

PRINCETON
UNIVERSITY
PRESS
◎◎
*Princeton
and Oxford*

Published by Princeton University Press, 41 William Street, Princeton, New Jersey 08540

In the United Kingdom: Princeton University Press, 3 Market Place, Woodstock, Oxfordshire OX20 1SY

LIBRARY OF CONGRESS CATALOGING-IN-PUBLICATION DATA
Vendler, Helen Hennessy.
  Invisible listeners : lyric intimacy in Herbert, Whitman, and Ashbery / Helen Vendler.
      p. cm.
  Includes bibliographical references and index.
  ISBN-13: 978-0-691-11618-1 (cloth : acid-free paper)
  ISBN-10: 0-691-11618-0 (cloth : acid-free paper)
      1. American poetry—History and criticism.   2. Intimacy (Psychology) in literature.   3. Whitman, Walt, 1819–1892—Criticism and interpretation.   4. Herbert, George, 1593–1633—Criticism and interpretation.   5. Ashbery, John—Criticism and interpretation.
  6. Lyric poetry—History and criticism.   7. Authors and readers—United States.   8. Authors and readers—England.   9. Reader-response criticism.   10. God in literature.   I. Title.
PS310.I57V46 2005
811'.0409—dc22   2005043967

British Library Cataloging-in-Publication Data is available

This book has been composed in Adobe Jenson Pro

Printed on acid-free paper. ∞

pup.princeton.edu

Printed in the United States of America

10 9 8 7 6 5 4 3 2

For Killian and Céline

> Within what we permit,
> Within the actual, the warm, the near,
> So great a unity, that it is bliss,
> Ties us to those we love.

—WALLACE STEVENS, "Esthétique du Mal"

Q. Whom do you write for?

A. You know what Stravinsky said to that? [Robert Craft] puts the same question to Stravinsky and he says "for myself and the probable alter ego."

—*Conversations with Joseph Brodsky,*
ed. Cynthia L. Haven

Contents

Acknowledgments

I am grateful to the Princeton University Press for inviting me to give the Farnum Lectures on which this small book is based, and to two editors at the Press, Mary Murrell, who guided the book at its inception, and Hanne Winarsky, who brought it to its conclusion. The hospitality of the Press and the Department of English made my visit to Princeton a very pleasant one. I thank the anonymous readers of the manuscript, who raised significant questions that affected the final form of these chapters. It was the poet Alan Williamson who, some decades ago, when I expressed some skepticism about Ashbery, sat me down on the spot and made me read "The Skaters"; without that timely intervention, my subsequent writing on Ashbery, including the chapter here, might not have come about. My assistant, Alicia Peralta, put my manuscript into the proper form for the Press, and I owe her thanks for that as well as for her meticulous assistance in library research. Finally, and always, I feel gratitude to those who have taught me, either in person or by their books, to be a better reader of the poets considered here: these include the late Elsie Duncan-Jones, Wynn Thomas, Bonnie Costello, and John Shoptaw. My beloved grandchildren, to whom this book is affectionately dedicated, will I hope find my voice in it when they grow up.

Invisible Listeners

INTRODUCTION Invisible Listeners

◉◉ The chapters of this book investigate the odd practice by which certain poets address their poems, in whole or in part, to someone they do not know and cannot set eyes on, their invisible listener. George Herbert speaks to God; Walt Whitman to the reader in futurity; John Ashbery to a painter of the past. What are we to make of this choice of addressee? With many visible listeners presumably available—the beloved, the patron, the child, the friend—why does the poet feel he or she must hold a colloquy with an invisible other? And what is the ethical import of speaking to such a nonexistent being? To think about such a choice, we must look first at the more common sorts of address within the lyric.

In its usual form, the lyric offers us the representation of a single voice, alone, recording and analyzing and formulating and changing its mind. Although no one else is present in fact, the solitary poet is frequently addressing someone else, someone not in the room. It has even been claimed that apostrophe—literally, a turning away from one's strophe to address someone else—is the essence of the lyric (although there are many lyrics of solitary internal meditation that do not address another person; such a lyric is, as Arnold paradoxically said, a "dialogue of the mind with itself"). One possible absent addressee of lyric is a person whom the fictive speaker knows—a lover, a patron, a family member. The speaker of Shakespeare's sonnets may address the friend or the mistress; Donne may address his patron, Ben Jonson his dead son. This sort of human address could be called "horizontal": although the poet may adopt a tone of formal

1

respect (in the case of a patron) or one of adoring warmth (in the case of a lover), the addressee is, after all, merely another human being. But there exists also the "vertical" sort of address: in this case, the speaker's apostrophe is directed to a person or thing inhabiting a physically inaccessible realm conceived as existing "above" the speaker. The vertically situated addressee may be a god (Christian or classical) or a nightingale or a Grecian urn, and may be situated in Heaven, on Parnassus, or on a Platonic plane where Truth and Beauty are one. The tone adopted by the speaker in vertical apostrophe rises above the level of respect shown to a worldly patron or the veneration shown toward a beloved, and manifests a humility suitable to a speaker addressing the divine.

The loneliness experienced when one lacks an adequate relation to others is mentioned by many poets. "This is my letter," says Emily Dickinson, "to the World / That never wrote to Me." The painful asymmetry of the relation between expressive poet and indifferent audience compels the continuous production of her letters to the silent world. "Where art thou friend, whom I shall never see?" asks Hopkins, estranged from both family and fellow students by his conversion to Roman Catholicism. Hopkins imagines two locations for the permanently invisible friend. Perhaps he is only somewhere else in the contemporary world—"sunder'd from my sight in the age that is"—but more probably, given the unconventionality of Hopkins's character and verse, the friend remains the "far-off promise of a time to be":

> Where art thou friend, whom I shall never see,
> Conceiving whom I must conceive amiss?
> Or sunder'd from my sight in the age that is
> Or far-off promise of a time to be;
> Thou who canst best accept the certainty
> That thou hadst borne proportion in my bliss,

That likest in me either that or this,—
Oh! even for the weakness of the plea
That I have taken to plead with,— if the sound
Of God's dear pleadings have as yet not moved thee,—
And for those virtues I in thee have found,
Who say that had I known I had approved thee,—
For these, make all the virtues to abound,—
No, but for Christ who hath foreknown and loved thee.[1]

Although Hopkins's invisible friend more probably lives in the future—"a time to be"—than in the present, the poet adopts toward him a tone of plangent present intimacy, confident that the friend would like in him one or another trait. At the same time, Hopkins recognizes the "weakness of the plea" of recommending religious conversion on the basis of a putative intimacy conceived over an impassable gulf of time. The extreme hunger of the present casts its desire for intimacy forward, imagining a society that could produce a companion who would bear proportion in the poet's bliss.

In these passages, Dickinson and Hopkins convert the normal intimate address to a known other into a rarefied form—intimate address to an unknown human other. What all lyrics of apostrophe, horizontal or vertical, offer us are tones of voice through which they represent, by analogy, various relations resembling those that we know in life. Lyrics can replicate the tenderness of a parent, the jealousy of a lover, the solicitude of a friend, the humility of a sinner. Such lyrics reveal the social relations in which the speaker is enmeshed, and they often embed within themselves the social norms embodied in various institutions such as the family, the church, or courtly love. But what is the poet to do who wants not to *express* such relations but to *redefine* them, who yearns, for example, to adopt a more intimate relation to God than that offered by the church, who intends to model an erotic relation between men not yet sanctioned by society, or who seeks an aesthetic identity currently unfashionable among living artists, but visibly present in the past? The intrinsic and constitutive ability of the lyric to create intimacy is perhaps most striking when the object of intimacy can never be humanly seen or known, yet can be humanly addressed. In such a case, the unseen other becomes an unseen listener, anchoring the voice of the poet as it issues into the otherwise vacant air.

I will here be reflecting on the creation of intimacy with the invisible in the work of three poets. George Herbert, not finding in conventional prayer adequate verbal expressions of his relation to the divine, invents a new constellation of tones and structures with which to address a God who, though sometimes seeming to reside above the poet in an eternity inaccessible to human thought, more often resides (in the horizontal plane) not only within the poet's room but inside his heart, and, in an extraordinary way, inside poetry itself. Walt Whitman, not finding in conventional social intercourse, or in the lyrics he knew, the intimate relation with a man that he yearns for, invents an invisible comrade-reader in futurity somewhat resembling Hopkins's imagined friend. But whereas in Hopkins that friend appears only once, in Whitman the ideal addressee is evoked constantly throughout the first three editions of *Leaves of Grass*, creating and sustaining an intimacy that more and more casts itself from present hope into future dream. In *Self-Portrait in a Convex Mirror*, John Ashbery, not finding a fellow-artist of his own time who shares his aesthetic of partial distortion accompanying figuration, addresses the sixteenth-century Mannerist painter Francesco Parmigianino not as someone dead but as someone alive and listening. In fantasizing new personal relations not available in the conventional present, the poets intimate a Utopia in which such closeness would be an accessible part of the known—where the sinner would find unforeseeable tones of intimacy toward a loving

4

Savior, where society would allow openly demonstrated love between men, where artists—no longer feeling obliged to align themselves exclusively with a figurative or an abstract school—would
recognize that all art bends reality into aesthetic abstraction and
distortion.

How does a poet make real, in language and in form, both the
invisible addressee and his relation to that addressee—or, to put it
differently—how is the "intimacy effect" produced on the page?[2] As
I've said, creation of this sort of intimacy springs from a fundamen-
tal loneliness, forcing the author to conjure up a listener unavailable
in actual life. And yet something in the current social world must
help to create in verse the image of the ideal listener. The poet may
look for textual evidence of the hoped-for listener (Herbert searches
the Bible in this way for hints of a God more familiar than distant);
or the poet may stabilize and prolong on the page a love that in actual life has been transitory (Whitman's reader-in-futurity satis-
fies the erotic connection that, in life, Whitman found fleeting).
When there is nothing in current life that can give hints of the intimate link for which the poet longs, the envisaged new addressee
may be summoned up by a reaction against the present: Ashbery, a
twentieth-century artist unable, at the moment of writing *Self-Portrait*,
to find a congenial aesthetic among his contemporaries, discovers
(with surprise, relief, and joy) a painter of the past demonstrating
an intermediate manner of composition—partly representative, partly
abstractly distorted—similar to his own.

Although in the usual lyric the speaker is alone, this solitude
does not mean that he is without a social ambiance. It means only
that his current social conditions are presented as they are reflected
on in solitude, embodied not in "live" interaction with other persons
but in lexical and intellectual reference. The necessary solitude of
the lyric speaker has caused socially oriented critics to conclude
that lyric lacks information about their fields of interest: the clash

of classes, the domestic and political mediations of sexuality, the fabric of community. On this view, once a speaker is alone in his room, nothing interactively interesting can happen, nothing of social value can be articulated.[3]

It is of course the poet-speaker's own ethical choices that become articulated in the language creating the elastic space between himself and the other. With each cast of his imagination, as it formulates an encounter with the divine, Herbert chooses the sort of God he desires; the qualities of that God, as He is brought into view, are extrapolated from Herbert's own best ethical principles. When an unsuitable ethical principle is proposed by the poet (that God should find suitable "employment" for His priest, or that the soul's "dust and sin" should find condign punishment), Herbert's God finds ways to set the errant principle gently, but firmly, aside. With each conceiving of his desired comrade Whitman, too, creates an ethics: his ethics not only ratifies extant democratic principles (liberty, equality, fraternity), but, by tone and metaphor, carries such principles to unexpected extensions—imagining liberty of gender-choice in lovers, or an equality between himself and the divine, or the fraternity between himself and a "common prostitute."

In the chapters that follow, I will say relatively little about the ethical dimension in Herbert and Whitman, since their ethical positions are frequently outspoken ones. Ashbery, however, is not usually thought of as a poet with ethical concerns. Yet in his command of volatile tonality he succeeds in suggesting a gamut of ethical relations, from the hostile to the dismissive, from the amorous to the self-denying. Beyond the formal domain there is the fictive one, and there, as Ashbery creates a relation to a past artist, we see embodied, in moving delineation, the qualities of envy, love, ambition, fear, and even enmity that motivate the poet's relation to his precursor. Ashbery's elaboration in his poem of an aesthetic relation across centuries is as lonely and full-bodied as the Parmigianino painting from which it departs: each of these two works of art is conceived as a self-portrait alive to its own reception by another.

Considerations of the ethical importance of literature usually ground themselves in case histories drawn from such socially oriented texts as Greek tragedies or complex novels. The lyric, however, conveys ethical import less by narration of character in action than by believable tonalities (which may be of any sort—appealing or truculent or repellent), tonalities that are invented and expended as the poet structures and elaborates the emotions of his fantasy. As the lyric contrives its web of relation with another person (or with a thing—an urn or a nightingale—imagined as an addressable being), the filaments it flings (to use Whitman's metaphor) catch at that "somewhere" (or someone) implicit in all poetic address.[4] The tones summoned up characterize not only their utterer but also his relation to his addressee, creating on the page the nature of the ties between them.

Julia Kristeva analogizes intimacy to the discourse of the psychoanalytic hour,[5] but the discourse projected outwards by the lyric poet is of a verbal deliberateness unavailable to either analysand or analyst. The poet's "written speech" must obey (as discourse directed to an analyst does not) laws of structural and formal poetics.[6] And these, because they are inherited from the past, may bear an equivocal or problematic relation to the revisionary ethical formulation that the poet aims to fashion. Insofar as every human relation-of-two entails an ethical dimension (of justice, estimation, reciprocity, sympathy), so, too, does every lyric representation of the linkage of two persons. This ethical dimension, though self-evident in novelists or dramatists or even lyric poets addressing other human beings, is even more provocative in the poetry of the invisible listener. Can the projection of models of verbal intimacy—one of lyric's greatest powers—be considered as a form of ethically serious activity?

I will be examining how the poet's strange imagined relation with a listener who is invisible—either because he is divine, or because he exists only in the future, or because he is long dead—can be made psychologically credible, emotionally moving, and aesthetically powerful. But it is not only a neutral depiction of a relation that the poet has in mind: he aims to establish in the reader's imagination a more admirable ethics of relation, one more desirable than can be found at present on the earth. Such is the Utopian will of these poets, as desire calls into being an image of possibility not yet realized in life, but—it is postulated—realizable. This possibility is brought to life on the page with a tenderness, wonder, and confidence that are borrowed from the closest moments of intimacy in life. Intimacy with the invisible is an intimacy with hope. Reading these poems, we take a step forward in conceiving a better intimacy—religious, sexual, or aesthetic—than we have hitherto known.

ONE George Herbert and God

૭૭ I hope to describe here George Herbert's startling accomplishment in revising the conventional vertical address to God until it approaches the horizontal address to an intimate friend. This original intuition was not enacted immediately in Herbert's writing, though it was always longed for. Herbert inherits ways of thinking about, and addressing, God from two chief sources, the Bible and the liturgy.[1] Both in the Old Testament and the New, Herbert finds anecdotes of intimacy with God: there was a moment, the poet recalls with nostalgia, when God was so familiar with his people that he had to beseech Moses to let him alone (Exod. 32: 9–14):

> Sweet were the dayes, when thou didst lodge with Lot,
> Struggle with Jacob, sit with Gideon,
> Advise with Abraham, when thy power could not
> Encounter Moses' strong complaints and mone:
> > Thy words were then, *Let me alone.*
>
> One might have sought and found thee presently
> At some fair oak, or bush, or cave, or well:
> Is my God this way? No, they would reply:
> He is to Sinai gone, as we heard tell:
> > List, ye may hear great Aarons bell.
> > > "Decay" [99][2]

In this formulation, what separates Herbert from familiarity with God is his belatedness in time. Though God still dwells in the human heart, He is now pinched and straitened there, Herbert says, by Sin and Satan, and His love has closeted itself and continues to retreat. Only at the Last Judgment will it once again exert its great heat, "And calling *Justice,* all things burn." Intimacy and full warmth are things lost, now that we no longer live in the Patriarchal age; and God's eventual wrath seems at present more evident than his love. Here, intimacy with God is sought, rather than found.

In other poems, what separates Herbert from intimacy with God is not time, but space—a vertical space that can be bridged, perhaps, but only temporarily. In two poems—one in Latin, one in English—Herbert imagines the potential bridge to Heaven as one made of sunbeams. In the third of his nineteen poems on his mother's death (1627), he first imagines the sun as able to let his Heaven-dwelling mother down to earth again by means of one of its rays; but supposing this impossible, he implores the sun to multiply its rays so that the son, twining his hand in them, may climb up to where his mother is.[3] This "silk twist" ("The Pearl") of sunbeams let down from Heaven reappears in "Mattens," as Herbert prays (in his own imaginative version of a portion of the Divine Office) that the morning light may show forth to him both the Creator and his work:

> Teach me Thy love to know;
> That this new light, which now I see,
> May both the work and workman show:
> Then by a sunne-beam I will climb to Thee.
>
> "Mattens" [63]

The vertical distance from God is bridged in "Artillerie" by a shooting star (the night version, one could say, of the sunbeam), a burning chastisement sent from Heaven to remind the neglectful Herbert of his religious duties. Herbert plaintively retorts to God that he himself has "starres and shooters too": "My tears and prayers night and day do wooe, / And work up to thee; yet thou dost refuse" [139]. It is a poignant loneliness desiring fuller intimacy that generates such vertical bridges as the sunbeam and the shooting star. They represent a model (well known to us all) in which a distressing distance is felt within intimacy; the impulse to merge entirely is implied, but distance cannot at the present be made to disappear.

In his longing for entire intimacy, Herbert sometimes becomes unable to tolerate any distance at all. "Clasping of Hands" imagines a fused identity repudiating altogether those first- and second-person adjectives "mine" and "thine." Although "Clasping of Hands"—taking its title from a gesture of human friendship—begins with a statement of mutual possession, "Lord, thou art mine, and I am thine," it ends, in its last line, praying that its former adjectives may be abrogated, that some ineffable new state (at present only negatively describable) can be attained, when there will be "no Thine and Mine":

> O be mine still! still make me thine!
> Or rather make no Thine and Mine!
>
> [157]

This ecstatic merging can hardly take place in the fallen present, and Herbert must forsake the hope of annihilating all distance between himself and God. Still, the fact of distance, once postulated, provokes the fear that there may be no available bridge, that the sinner will be abandoned to a state of perpetual estrangement, as in "The Pilgrimage." The weary pilgrim—after passing the cave of desperation and the rock of Pride, leaving Fancy's meadow, getting through Care's copse, and being robbed in the wild of Passion— believes he has at last come to Zion's hill, where, by climbing vertically to the top he will find God:

> At length I got unto the gladsome hill,
> Where lay my hope,
> Where lay my heart; and climbing still,

11

When I had gain'd the brow and top,
A lake of brackish waters on the ground
Was all I found.

With that abash'd and struck with many a sting
Of swarming fears,
I fell, and cry'd, Alas my King!
Can both the way and end be tears?

[142]

The pilgrim of this poem never does reach his goal; and the distant "King" addressed here never embraces his subject. With such a "King," intimacy has become, it would seem, unattainable.

How is Herbert to formulate and make real the intimacy he desires, given the obstacles of time and space, Sin and Satan, and the inscrutability and distance of a sovereign God? If God is no longer familiarly with us on earth, as he was in the days of Abraham, He might at least, the poet thinks (in a rather unsatisfactory model of intimacy), be an intermittent guest in our house; yet if He does not make "a constant stay" we feel the absence of a consistent intimacy with Him. The inconstancy of God's felt presence is the source of much of Herbert's pain in *The Temple*: at the same time, paradoxically, it is the occasion for some of Herbert's most intimate tones of reproach:

Whither away delight?
Thou cam'st but now; wilt thou so soon depart,
And give me up to night?
For many weeks of lingring pain and smart
But one half houre of comfort to my heart?

"The Glimpse" [154]

If distance and intermittent glimpses will not yield the desired closeness, Herbert will try to find winged helpers to aid him in overcoming the vertical distance. He proposes to Sunday (the day of the Lord) that together they "flie hand in hand to heav'n" ["Sunday," 77]; he says to church-music, "If I travell in your companie, / You know the way to heavens doore" ["Church-music," 66]; and he urges a star to refine him with its fire and then bear him back to its native Heaven where his Savior's face is crowned with beams of light,

> That so among the rest I may
> Glitter, and curle, and winde as they:
> That winding is their fashion
> Of adoration.
>
> "The Starre" [74]

But intimacy with a heavenly companion, whether Sunday, music, or star, is no substitute for intimacy with God Himself. Perhaps God can be brought nearer, Herbert reflects, by reimagining Him not as King or Lord, but as parent.[4] In this model God more closely resembles a mother than a father ("From thee all pitie flows. / Mothers are kinde, because thou art, / And dost dispose / To them a part" ["Longing," 148]. In one of his early poems, "Perseverance," Herbert implicitly represents himself as an infant clinging to the breast of a maternal God, separated by no distance at all:

> Onely my soule hangs on thy promisses
> With face and hands clinging unto thy brest,
> Clinging and crying, crying without cease,
> Thou art my rock, thou art my rest.
>
> [205][5]

This kindly parent-figure (whom Herbert usually represents as male) is dulcet and tender, issuing reproofs of only the mildest sort. In "The Collar," the Lord has patiently listened without interrupting as the frustrated poet "rav'd and grew more fierce and wilde / At

every word." Instead of defending His own actions or rebuking the
sinner, the Lord merely calls to His straying son:

> But as I rav'd and grew more fierce and wilde
> > At every word,
> > Me thoughts I heard one calling, *Child*!
> > And I reply'd, *My Lord.*

> [153–54]

Although God seems to style Himself a parent by addressing the
poet as "Child," the ashamed child does not dare to claim the prof-
fered filial relation: he replies not "Father," but "My Lord." When
Herbert's own heart is in better order, as in another of his rewrit-
ings of a portion of the Divine Office, "Even-song," he can wonder-
ingly see, in "the God of love," not a "Lord," but a gentle parent reas-
suring human children as they fall asleep:

> > Yet still thou goest on,
> > And now with darknesse closest wearie eyes,
> > > Saying to man, *It doth suffice*:
> > > Henceforth repose; your work is done.

> > > I muse which shows more love,
> > The day or night; that is the gale, this th' harbour;
> > > That is the walk, and this the arbour;
> > > Or that the garden, this the grove.
> > > My God, thou art all love:
> > > Not one poore minute 'scapes thy breast,
> > > But brings a favour from above;
> > And in this love, more than in bed, I rest.

> [64]

When Herbert can feel that God is "all love," his work attains in
tone, and exemplifies, the intimacy he craves.

The word "love" becomes for Herbert a talisman of mutuality. Because it testifies to a right disposition of the poet's heart, it can enter into a chiasmus of near-symmetrical relation with God, where divine love and human love touch and overlap:

> Thy power and love, my love and trust
> Make one place ev'ry where.
>
> "The Temper (I)" [55]

The word "love" here stands for an identity of feeling. It renders God's love comprehensible by analogy with Herbert's own, while still distinguishing—as "Clasping of Hands" did not—the two participants, one of whom extends a benign "power" while the other responds with "trust." Even when Herbert imagines a symmetry of love, he does not feel that he can use the two usual active verbs of this mutual relation—"I love you," "You love me"—but rather testifies solely, as in "A True Hymn," to his own feelings, wherein he finds not only his own love given to God—"O, *could I love!*"—but also love received from God: "[I am] *Loved.*" God has reason to complain, the poet has said, if a verse, though it rhymes, is motivated by no inner devotion; but if the supplicant's heart be moved, even if his verse is inferior, nothing is wanting to the intimacy:

> . . . if th'heart be moved,
> Although the verse be somewhat scant,
> God doth supplie the want.
> As, when th' heart sayes (sighing to be approved)
> O, *could I love!* and stops: God writeth, *Loved.*
>
> [168]

Because the divinely inscribed "*Loved*" not only fills out the verse line but also completes the rhyme, we see that when the poet's heart fills with love, God steps in to make the "somewhat scant" verse perfect in all respects—in thought, in rhythm, and in rhyme. In this

15

model of intimacy, friends intuit each other's unspoken desire and fulfill it without being asked. One friend is the completion—in meaning, in surge of feeling, and in consonance—of the other. The presence of the invisible listener is made palpable on Herbert's page by God's participation in their jointly written poem.

Herbert's most credible dramatic model is one of almost horizontal intimacy with the God who writes, or speaks, as a friend.[6] God as a parent, however solicitous, remains in an asymmetrical and vertically distant relation to the soul, adult to child. Only in the relation of adult to adult can Herbert find a more satisfying image of intimacy, and create a humanly realized divine actor within the drama of salvation. Friendship may have become Herbert's best model for intimacy with God because it was the adult relation he most prized. Friendship is therefore also the model by which he judges his own ethical shortcomings in his doings with God, as he confesses in "Unkindnesse." With respect to earthly friends he makes sure (he says) that whatever he intends will not damage the friendship; he will defend his friend "from the least spot or thought of blame"; he freely gives to a friend in need; and he puts the friend's interest above his own. But in his relations with God, he fears, the reverse is true. Each stanza of "Unkindnesse" ends with the poet's disgrace, as he not only treats God worse than he does his friends, he treats Him—in the shamefaced last line—worse than he treats his foes:

> I would not use a friend, as I use Thee. . . .
> I could not use a friend, as I use Thee. . . .
> I cannot use a friend, as I use Thee. . . .
> Nor would I use a friend, as I use Thee. . . .
> Yet use I not my foes, as I use Thee.[7]

> [93–94]

It is not surprising, then, that Herbert—who finds in Jesus-the-friend a model of what could be his own best self—in certain moments of writing encounters God with no hint of distance. In vindicating the act of writing poetry, Herbert declares that although verse may be held in worldly contempt, yet it is of inestimable value in enabling intimacy with God and a felt sense of receiving His favors. When writing verse, says the poet to God in "The Quidditie," "I am with thee, and *most take all*":

> My God, a verse is not a crown,
> No point of honour, or gay suit,
> No hawk, or banquet, or renown,
> Not a good sword, nor yet a lute:
>
> It cannot vault, or dance, or play;
> It never was in *France* or *Spain*;
> Nor can it entertain the day
> With my great stable or demain:
>
> It is no office, art, or news,
> Nor the Exchange, or busie Hall;
> But it is that which while I use
> I am with thee, and *most take all*.

[69–70]

Poetry is not possessions, or actions, or institutions: the negative mode of definition, familiar from theology, could hardly be carried further than it is in these first ten lines of concession, followed by the "but" that tips the balance with its single extraordinary and complicated formulation: a verse is that thing which, when I engage in its exercise, situates me in intimacy with God, makes me possessed of every good. "I am with thee" does not abrogate difference of persons, as does the close of "Clasping of Hands"; but it dares to suggest a union of friends, a state well defined in our normal lives and therefore available for projection onto the plane of the divine.

In the poems in which God, in the person of Jesus, speaks as a

contemporary friend, we find some of Herbert's most winningly intimate lines, as he emboldens himself to write dialogue for Jesus to
speak. The paradigm of such poems is "Love unknown," which opens
with the defining Herbertian confiding tone, as the narrator says to
an unspecified interlocutor, "Deare Friend, sit down, the tale is long
and sad." The naïve narrator has no idea that his interlocutor-Friend
is Jesus. Although he assumes that in the Friend he has a willing listener, he doubts that the Friend has any power to extricate him from
the abuse he has suffered at the hands of the servants of his Master:

> Deare Friend, sit down, the tale is long and sad:
> And in my faintings I presume your love
> Will more complie than help.

As the narrator recounts the insults wreaked on his heart, the Friend
offers mild critical observations, always phrased subjectively with the
clause, "I fear." His heart—says the indignant narrator—was thrown
into a fountain of blood where it was washed and wrung ("the very
wringing yet / Enforceth tears"); at this, the Friend merely remarks,
Your heart was foul, I fear. The heart was then thrown into a cauldron:
"[T]he man . . . / Threw my heart into the scalding pan; My heart,
that brought [my offering] (do you understand?) / The offerers
heart." To this pained insistence, the Friend merely repeats his previous comment, changing only an adjective. If a "foul" heart perhaps
needed washing, a hard heart might have needed melting: *Your heart
was hard, I fear.* The narrator then recounts, with complaining resentment, that he found his bed stuffed with painful "thoughts, / I would
say *thorns.*" He becomes pitiful:

> Deare, could my heart not break,
> When with my pleasures ev'n my rest was gone?

The Friend replies with another temperate adjective: *Your heart was
dull, I fear.* At this third gentle suggestion that the "abuse" commanded

by the Master was warranted, the narrator at last acknowledges his faults and recognizes his spiritual sloth. Finally, the interlocutor—so laconic until this closing moment—speaks at length, addressing the narrator in his turn as "Friend." In his comment, he reveals the gracious adjectives that will reverse the previously *foul, hard, dull* condition of the narrator's heart:

> *Truly, Friend,*
>
> *For ought I heare, your Master shows to you*
> *More favours then you wot of. Mark the end.*
> *The Font did onely, what was old, renew:*
> *The Caldron suppled, what was grown too hard:*
> *The Thorns did quicken, what was grown too dull:*
> *All did but strive to mend, what you had marr'd.*
> *Wherefore be cheer'd, and praise him to the full*
> *Each day, each houre, each moment of the week,*
> *Who fain would have you be new, tender, quick.*

[129–31]

This Friend—so understanding yet so certain in his interpretations—answers the narrator's protest with instruction, not reproof; blames ignorance rather than sin; suggests that the narrator has received not abuse but "more favours than you wot of "; and displaces querulous impatience with benign result: "*Mark the end.*" If your Master wants for you only the best—that you should be "*new, tender, quick*"—surely your own wishes for yourself must tend in that direction as well; and if ordeals (the Font, the Cauldron, the Thorns) were the difficult means, the end at least is fair. The gentle revelations of the Friend—reiterating his earlier adjectives in the form "*old*" (kindly substituted for the harsher "foul"), "*hard,*" and "*dull*" and then reversing them with the verbs "*did renew,*" "*suppled,*" and "*did quicken*"—mimics the action of the master in "magically" transforming the former heart into one "*new, tender, quick.*" To put off the old man of sin for the new man of grace, to put off the dullness of spiritual death for the quickness of eternal life, is the convincing process described by the Friend. What might seem an accusation—the Friend's remark to the narrator that "*you had marr'd*" the original "*new, tender, quick*" soul you once had—is actually neutral description, on a par with the "*did renew*" and "*suppled*" and "*did quicken*" of the revised narration. The Friend speaks as if renewing and suppling and quickening are all recurrrent natural processes, cycles in which marring is mended, foulness is renewed, hardness is suppled, and dullness is quickened. He names and justifies the processes; he does not reproach. He urges cheerfulness and praise, not penance or remorse. The compassionate Friend confirms to his newly burnished narrator-friend that he is now in the desirable and enjoyable state of being "*new, tender, quick*."

Jesus' function in "Love unknown" is that of a *viva voce* interpreter of the narrator's complaints, making love unknown into love known. Herbert conceives of his reader, I think, in terms of comparable intimacy, as the poems of *The Temple* say to us, in effect, "Deare Friend, sit down, the tale is long and sad." Through Jesus' example here, Herbert offers us a model of how to listen to an intimate friend who is suffering. Jesus listens patiently to the whole self-pitying tale; his comments are, though interpretative, not direct reproofs; not a global "you," he says, but an aspect of you—"your heart"—has faltered. Jesus' comments are brief, kind-hearted, and tentatively phrased. Only toward the end, when his third remark has produced an acknowledgment of fault from the narrator, does Jesus venture on his heartening post-facto observations on the happy end and the improved state of the narrator, merely alluding to the fact that the narrator had blighted a better state—"*what you had marr'd.*" Although the Friend is more clear-sighted than the narrator, he addresses him not condescendingly but reassuringly. Divine intimacy—in this playlet-model—abstains from condemnation, remains within a descriptive neutrality in clarifying the sinner's predicament, urges a happier state of mind, and reveals that there was meaning in the ordeal undergone. We recognize Herbert's Pauline source: love is patient and kind.[8] And the modern reader may, in being shown Herbert's forbearing Jesus, reflect that Herbert has anticipated the modern notion of the ideal therapist—suggesting what a credible human presence Herbert can create on the page.

But there are even better moments of intimacy to be had, and to learn from, than the asymmetrical, however gentle, moment of ethical instruction of the mistaken novice by a more able interpreter. These better moments are formulated in the last two poems of *The Temple*, "Heaven" [188] and "Love (III)" [188–89]. In the first of these—an echo-poem—Herbert suggests that to be an intimate friend is to answer, with improvements, a speaker's questions, using, to his surprise, his own syllables to do so. Here, the speaker (unlike the narrator of "Love unknown") is always "right" in his phonemes (his heart is in the right place), but he is not yet sure of his own future destiny, and so must be confirmed in his righteousness by having God's Word—sounding from the immortal leaves of the Bible—replay (and wittily revise) his very words, in a reiterated celestial approval:

Heaven

O who will show me those delights on high?
   Echo. I.
Thou Echo, thou art mortall, all men know.
   Echo. No.
Wert thou not born among the trees and leaves?
   Echo. Leaves.
What leaves are they? impart the matter wholly.
   Echo. Holy.

Are holy leaves the Echo then of blisse?
>   *Echo.*   Yes.
Then tell me, what is that supreme delight?
>   *Echo.*   Light.
Light to the minde: what shall the will enjoy?
>   *Echo.*   Joy.
But are there cares and businesse with the pleasure?
>   *Echo.*   Leisure.
Light, joy, and leisure; but shall they persever?
>   *Echo.*   Ever.[9]

[188]

This exquisite poem incarnates a fantasy of perfect intimacy, in which the celestial Friend's mind musically echoes our own. We find nothing in the Friend's echo that was not first found in ourselves; and in our antiphony with the Friend we will find ourselves the same, but improved and approved.[10] This relation, like the one in "Love unknown," allows for a disparity of knowledge between the two Friends: *Echo* "knows more" than the speaker. This is perhaps a necessary aspect of intimacy for an intellectual such as Herbert: an intimate friend ideally would supply growth in knowledge as well as reciprocity in affection. "Heaven" is a poem of promises, but without the anguish of that earlier poem of promises, "Perseverance," which cried, "Onely my soul hangs on thy promises, / . . . Clinging and crying, crying without cease" [205]. In the poem "Heaven," the promises are explicit from the first line to the last: the soul will be shown the delights on high, the light, joy, and leisure that will persever, ever.

It might be thought that "Heaven" reaches the utmost model of intimacy, realistically preserving a duality (as "Clasping of Hands" did not) but intimating a chiming coincidence of mentalities and words. However, the intimacy of "Heaven" is intellectual and linguistic, pertaining to the soul rather than to the body (which is present only in the insubstantial "higher" sense of hearing). In Herbert's deepest investigation into the actions, gestures, and language of intimacy, the model he presents is that of physical and emotional sustenance in one, eating and drinking in the house of a Friend (whose name is immediately given as "Love"). Here, Herbert's speaker is a guest; he first encounters the deliberately ungendered Friend as the host at the door,[11] bidding welcome, gently putting aside the guest's protestations of physical and spiritual unworthiness, and—to the guest's determination to take the lowly place of servant—replying that his role is rather that of desired guest:

Love (III)

Love bade me welcome: yet my soul drew back,
    Guiltie of dust and sinne.
But quick-ey'd Love, observing me grow slack
    From my first entrance in,
Drew nearer to me, sweetly questioning
    If I lack'd any thing.

A guest, I answer'd, worthy to be here:
    Love said, You shall be he.
I, the unkinde, ungratefull? Ah my deare,
    I cannot look on thee.
Love took my hand, and smiling did reply,
    Who made the eyes but I?

Truth, Lord, but I have marr'd them: let my shame
    Go where it doth deserve.
And know you not, sayes Love, who bore the blame?
    My deare, then I will serve.

> You must sit down, sayes Love, and taste my meat.
> So I did sit and eat.
>
> [188–89][12]

In "Love (III)" as in "Heaven," the formal figure enacting intimacy is antiphony, but here Herbert presents antiphony of gesture as well as of language, as the following diagram of the back-and-forth movement of the poem will suggest. The actions and gestures on either side are rendered in italics:

Love (III)

Host	Guest
	Host ... *Guest*

Host

Love bade me welcome,

                               Guest

                         yet my soul drew back,
                    Guiltie of dust and sinne.

But quick-ey'd Love, *observing me grow slack*
                        From *my first entrance in,*

Drew nearer to me, sweetly questioning
    If I lack'd anything.

                        A guest, I answer'd, worthy to be here:

Love said, You shall be he.
                        I, the unkinde, ungratefull? Ah my deare,
                        I cannot look on thee.

Love took my hand, and smiling did reply,
    Who made the eyes but I?

                        Truth, Lord, but I have marr'd them: *let my shame*
                        Go where it doth deserve.

And know you not, *sayes Love, who bore the blame?*
                        My deare, then *I will serve.*

You must sit down, sayes Love, and taste my meat.
                        So I *did sit and eat.*

In this depiction of intimacy as a heavenly banquet, Love might seem to know more than the sinner (as did the interpreting Friend in "Love unknown" and the supplementing Echo in

"Heaven"); but as we think about the answers Love here supplies, we see that Love is merely reminding the Christian sinner of things he already knows. He knows, certainly, that God made him, eyes and all; and he knows "who bore the blame" for his sin. Love's smiling replies are not ones of instruction—after all, the saved soul, already admitted to the banquet of the just, knows all he needs to know. Rather, Love's remarks function as reassurance. Of course you are not "a guest worthy to be here," Love agrees, because no one can deserve Heaven; so that when the sinner says that what he lacks is "a guest . . . worthy to be here," Love answers not with "You are he," but rather with the ordaining words "You shall be he." Love's "shall be" (not, significantly, the "will be" of futurity) represents the salvific will of God and its efficacious means, the sanctifying power of the Holy Spirit. In this representation, as in "Heaven," the sinner will be improved while remaining himself: "You" and "worthy guest" are firmly joined in the copula of ordained identity—a copula of certainty, guaranteed by those promises on which Herbert has counted before. We are reminded—by the quiet of "So I did sit and eat"—of the firm "I am with thee, and *most take all*" that ended "The Quidditie."

"Love" (III) has sometimes been described as a poem mirroring the elaborate courtesies of the Renaissance court.[13] But courtesy is not intimacy; and ethical intimacy goes far deeper than courtesy. Love can sympathetically read the mind of the shamefaced sinner; Love is "quick-ey'd," observant of the guest's discomfort; Love extends the hand of genuine welcome, not merely that of courtesy. This Love, as a model of intimacy, goes beyond the disinterestedness of friendship, with its reciprocity of mutual good evoked as a model relation in "Unkindnesse." Love's generosity exceeds reciprocity; it is pressed down and running over; and in the end it substitutes for courtly reciprocity a humble service. The host, in a celestial rewriting of courtly manners, stands and serves, the sinner sits and eats.[14] Our great difficulty in accepting intimacy is acted out by the mortified sinner. In the end, he capitulates with the grateful monosyllables that are the sign of the inexpressible: "So I did sit and eat."

What is the attraction, to a poet of intimacy, of addressing or describing an invisible Friend? In actual worldly relations—and Herbert had close relations with his birth family, his wife and nieces, his friends and parishioners—there occur countless obstacles to intimacy: age, circumstance, illness, overwork. An invisible addressee or listener, by contrast, makes the poem resemble one of those "pure" problems posed by mathematics, where one assumes the absence of friction, or postulates an absolute vacuum, or inscribes a dimensionless point, or stipulates any number of other conditions impossible in reality. In the ether of the invisible, psychological models can be constructed unhindered by anything but the speaker's attitude toward the proposed relation, and so the conditions and hypotheses of intimacy, such as those we have seen, can be explored freely, and a heart-satisfying ethics of intimate relation can be suggested.

Besides his skill in inventing models of desirable human relations, Herbert's great achievement in the poetry of intimacy is the gamut of tones he brings to bear during his experiments. The quintessential Herbertian tone, as I have said, is one of intimate confiding, as in "Deare Friend, sit down, the tale is long and sad." But there are also hectic tones of rebellion, pleading tones of entreaty, wincing tones of shame, seductive tones of persuasion, angry tones of resentment, ecstatic tones of joy, brooding tones of depression, hopeful tones of interrogation. Herbert could be described as an ethnolinguist of the multiple tonalities available to intimate conversation. Nobody else, for example, has imagined so well in verse what the invisible God might say back to a rebellious soul. We have already seen some unobtrusive remarks of the invisible Friend, but the most extended conversation of the sinner with this Interlocutor comes in the moving little poem "Dialogue" [114–15]. In it, the resentful sinner reproaches Jesus for His delay in saving a striving soul such as himself:

Sweetest Saviour, if my soul
    Were but worth the having,
Quickly should I then controll
    Any thought of waving.
But when all my care and pains
Cannot give the name of gains
To thy wretch so full of stains,
What delight or hope remains?

The first half of the stanza is balanced in statement and rhyme: *If* (two lines rhyming *ab*), *then* (two lines repeating the *ab* rhyme). This format betokens rational thought and equilibrated argument. But the second half of the stanza—prefaced by the adversative "but"—rises in a crescendo of undeviating rhyme, *cccc*, forsaking altogether the pretense of balance. As the soul vents its aggrieved accusations. Jesus replies:

What, Child, is the balance thine,
    Thine the poise and measure?
If I say, Thou shalt be mine;
    Finger not my treasure.
What the gains in having thee
Do amount to, onely he,
Who for man was sold, can see;
That transferr'd th'accounts to me.

Jesus' tone in this stanza is one of "poise and measure" throughout, the tone of one balancing accounts in accordance with evidence only he can see. We recognize an emotional crescendo here in lines

5–7, matching and countering the speaker's own, but a competition in suffering is averted by Jesus' putting his own case in the third person, referring to himself as "*he,* / *Who for man was sold.*" The only departure from the measured tone is the introductory "What, Child": this is a Savior or parent, not an accountant, speaking. The Savior has yet to speak in the first person of his redemptive acts.

The sinner's answer to Jesus' rebuttal is casuistic and petulant: his first quatrain, the "balanced" one, is legalistic, and his second quatrain, with its crescendo on one rhyme, is dangerous to his salvation:

> But as I can see no merit,
> > Leading to this favour:
> So the way to fit me for it
> > Is beyond my savour.
> As the reason then is thine;
> So the way is none of mine:
> I disclaim the whole designe:
> Sinne disclaims and I resigne.

The disjunction of "mine" and "thine" is complete: the sinner and Sin now share the same verb. "I disclaim . . . : / Sinne disclaims." Herbert creates tones on the page with wonderful ingenuity, and much could be said about his verbal and syntactic means: in his quarrel with Jesus here, the sinner avails himself of both theological terms ("merit") and worldly ones ("favour"), and looks to his own "savour" (French: *savoir*) rather than to his "saviour" for the way to fit into Jesus' "designe." The speaker's tone is both self-serving and resentful, pretending to logic ("As . . . / so") while succumbing to angry emotion ("I disclaim . . . / I resigne"). The terrible implied copula— "I am Sin"—which underlies the identity-clauses "I disclaim . . . / Sinne disclaims" represents the utter surrender of the human will to the persuasions of sin. And yet Jesus refuses to accept that the sinner can "resigne" his "designe." Aware that His previous "rational" accounting has not convinced the sinner, Jesus offers an emotional reference to his sacrifice, this time in the first person, reminding the sinner of a true form of "resigning"—Jesus' own:

> *That is all, if that I could*
>   *Get without repining;*
> *And my clay, my creature, would*
>   *Follow my resigning:*
> *That as I did freely part*
> *With my glorie and desert,*
> *Left all joyes to feel all smart—*

As Jesus avails himself of the power of the stanzaic single-rhyme crescendo (*part . . . / desert . . . / smart*), recalling how he left the glories and joys of Heaven to suffer "*all smart,*" the recalcitrant soul is overcome with sorrow, and the poem ends with the sinner's pang—"Ah! no more: thou break'st my heart." This model of intimacy transcribes the emotional and intellectual tones of an intimate dispute, in which the "emotional" stanzas bracket the "logical" ones, and we hear the tones change in consequence. Jesus' last "crescendo" is missing its final line: what would he have said if the sinner had not interrupted him? "If only you would follow my resigning," says Jesus, and we might imagine the consequent of that supposition—given the necessary rhyme-sound—as something like the following, if Jesus had completed his stanza (I bracket the invented line):

> *That as I did freely part*
> *With my glorie and desert,*
> *Left all joys to feel all smart—*
> [*You in grief would yield your heart.*]

But the sinner, in a convincing sign of intimacy, "finishes" Jesus' sentence (and stanza and rhyme) for him—and the coincidence of

Jesus' (supposed, intuited) wish and the sinner's complying exclamation shows us the sinner's capitulation to his Saviour's aesthetic design as well as his ethical reciprocity in "resigning." In this quarrel of intimates, the sinner's reluctance produced Jesus' logic; Jesus' logic produced the sinner's counterlogic; and then Jesus' emotion produced the sinner's responsive emotion, a synchrony allowing the participants' tones to mirror each other in a common poignancy, and the poem to end on a completed rhyme.

The ethics of intimacy in "Dialogue" recommends that if one strategy of reconciliation (here, Jesus' third-person one) between persons fails, a genuine friend will try another (here, Jesus' first-person narrative) until minds meet. The perfect symmetries of the Herbertian poem of intimacy—the minuet of welcome and guilt at the heavenly banquet of "Love (III)," the reciprocal exchanges of "Heaven" and "Dialogue"—reveal how completely these poems represent "pure" cases, theoretical experiments in mutuality, yearning "horizontal" revisions of the soul's usual "vertical" distance from God in the conventional rhetoric of prayer.

By projecting what we know of the pains and difficulties of actual intimacy onto a symbolic plane of abstract modeling, Herbert composes a manual of instruction toward better forms of intimacy in the actual world. However, by sequestering his intimacy with the invisible from an intimacy admitting the sexual, Herbert sets limits to the tones he permits himself. Walt Whitman, to whom we next turn, takes up the intimacy of friend and friend, projects it onto the future, and sexualizes it in a fashion both intense and equivocal, requiring a different set of models and tones from those we have seen in the poetry of George Herbert.

TWO   Walt Whitman and the
        Reader-in-Futurity

◉◉ Whitman certainly began not as a poet interested in the invisible but rather as a poet of strong bodily response expressed in a daring language of physicality. In the 1855 *Leaves of Grass* he invents a poetry of far-reaching symbolic resource in its description of the conjunction of bodies, as in his strikingly original rendition of fellatio:

> . . . What is this flooding me, childhood or manhood. . . . and
>   the hunger that crosses the bridge between . . .
> The cloth laps a first sweet eating and drinking,
> Laps life-swelling yolks. . . . laps ear of rose-corn, milky and
>   just ripened:
> The white teeth stay, and the boss-tooth advances in darkness,
> And liquor is spilled on lips and bosoms by touching glasses,
>   and the best liquor afterward.
>   "The Sleepers" [*LG* 1855, lines 66–70; p. 726][1]

It was his early intimacies with other bodies that made possible for Whitman that intimacy of voice so intoxicating to lovers, as he revels in the first-person plural "we" that releases the sexual self from its physical loneliness. Bodily intimacy appears in the "we two" of the 1860 *Enfans d'Adam* and *Calamus* poems, as Whitman joins himself to another to become "we two boys together clinging" on the open road, or, more powerfully, the "we two" who, when together, equal the whole created universe. "We are Nature," says the speaker of himself and his lover, as they undergo, in their

31

sexual companionship, multiple metamorphoses into essences both inanimate and animate:

> We become plants, trunks, foliage, roots, bark,
> We are bedded in the ground, we are rocks. . . .
> We prowl fang'd and four-footed in the woods, we spring
>   on prey,
> We are two clouds forenoons and afternoons driving
>   overhead,
> We are seas mingling, we are two of those cheerful waves
>   rolling over each other and interwetting each other,
> We are what the atmosphere is, transparent, receptive,
>   pervious, impervious. . . .
> We have circled and circled till we have arrived home again,
>   we two,
> We have voided all but freedom and all but our own joy.
>   "We Two, How Long We Were Fool'd" [p. 92–93]

This companionate physical intimacy is so necessary that without it, as another *Calamus* poem tells us, the poet fears he would not be able to write his poems:

> I saw in Louisiana a live-oak growing,
> All alone stood it and the moss hung down from the
>   branches,
> Without any companion it grew there uttering joyous leaves
>   of dark green,
> And its look, rude, unbending, lusty, made me think of
>   myself,
> But I wonder'd how it could utter joyous leaves standing alone
>   there without its friend near, for I knew I could not.
>   "I Saw in Louisiana a Live-Oak Growing" [p. 108]

Only after the physical fails does Whitman become a poet of intimacy with the invisible. Sometimes unable to secure, and always unable to sustain, actual sexual intimacy, Whitman is driven to invent an intimacy with the unseen; the poet is cast toward the lover-in-futurity by the faithlessness of the lover-in-the-present. The heartbreak that generates an invisible lover to replace the visible one is seen most clearly in the 1860 lyric "Hours Continuing Long" [520], a poem suppressed by Whitman from all subsequent editions of *Leaves of Grass*. Forsaken by his actual lover, the speaker, distracted and ashamed, withdraws "to a lonesome and unfrequented spot, seating myself, leaning my face in my hands." In these "sullen and suffering hours" he wonders "if other men have the like [hours] out of the like feelings?" As his misery seeks company, he reduces the number of men potentially resembling him to a single one:

> Is there even one other like me—distracted—his friend, his
> lover, lost to him?

And that other conjectured man, also a forsaken lover, is then made into a reader of Whitman's own poem:

> Does he see himself reflected in me? In these hours, does he
> see the face of his hours reflected?

Two forms of intimacy are conjured up here—a subjective psychological one ("himself reflected in me") and a more objective representational one ("In these hours, does he see the face of his hours reflected?"). Whitman is not yet directly addressing this imagined other who might not only resemble him but become his reader, nor is he yet projecting this alter ego into a far-off future: the hope of finding an actual lover, permeating the 1855 *Leaves of Grass*, still lingers in the 1860 edition. Yet between those two editions, in 1857, Whitman wrote a poem, "Full of life now" [116], in which he admits, with resignation, that the reader-in-futurity is the most likely lover he will have. He contrasts himself "full of life now, compact, visible" with the reader-in-futurity, who will at that time be the one who will be "compact, visible." On the supposition that two things equal to the same thing—being "compact, visible"—are equal to each other, the poet can construct an identity-exchange within a topological temporality in which past, present, and future tenses intermix, and indicative, subjunctive, and jussive moods intertwine. "Full of affection" (the original reading),[2] the poet speaks, imagining that his poems, after his death, continue to seek an envisaged comrade of the future who is in turn seeking them:

Full of life now, compact, visible,
I forty years old the eighty third year of the States,
To one a century hence or any number of centuries hence,
To you yet unborn these, seeking you.

When you read these I that was visible am become invisible,
Now it is you, compact, visible, realizing my poems,
     seeking me,
Fancying how happy you were if I could be with you and
     become your comrade;
Be it as if I were with you. (Be not too certain but I am now
     with you.)

The cost to the poet of finding an actual visible lover is the rendering of himself invisible. He becomes a ghost so that the camerado can become real. "Full of life now" bears three of the unmistakable marks of Whitmanian intimacy with the invisible: the poet's direct remarks to an invisible addressee of future time ("When you read these"); the poet's capacity to intuit his invisible listener's thoughts ("you . . . seeking me, / Fancying how happy you were if I could be with you"); and a faith in the mysterious power of poetry to convey presence ("Be not too certain but I am now with you"), the presence preceded by the ordaining power of the shaman: "Be it as if I were with you." Yearning toward someone who may not be born for some years or even hundreds of years hence is, as we have seen from the examples of Hopkins and Dickinson, a feeling not uncommon in lyric, but Whitman carries it further than any poet before or since. The problem is to give such a future listener tangible materiality on the page, and we will see Whitman experimenting with this task in many of the poems in *Leaves of Grass*.

Among the causes of Whitman's invention of a comrade-in-futurity, one was, as I have said, Whitman's love-disappointments in life, and his fear that without companionship he would cease to write. But his messianic tendencies also played a part in drawing his eyes toward the future, as did his belief in scientific and evolutionary progress. Whitmanian intimacy with the invisible, because it is so overdetermined, takes on many tonalities. A forsaken lover, speaking to an ideal lover yet to appear, does not use the same tone as a messiah speaking to his future followers, or a teacher to pupils as yet unborn, or a scientist publicly proclaiming natural events to come. "One of the roughs" speaking from the open road to an envisaged camerado takes yet another tone. The fluid Whitmanian self becomes, when oriented toward a future listener, unusually expansive and porous, and one of the attractions of Whitman's intimacy with the invisible is the discovery of the many Whitmans it brings forth ("I am large. . . . I contain multitudes. . . . / I resist anything better than my own diversity" ["Song of Myself," *LG* 1855, lines 1315–16; p. 347].

Whitman had begun his career as a balladeer and populist exhorter of others. But as he turned his gaze inward and discovered his true material—himself and his relation to the world and to language—he had to decide what tone to give the self-exposure he had promised in "You Felons on Trial in Courts" ("I exposé!"). Although he continued to resort, often enough, to either the homiletic tone of the preacher or the rhetorical tone of the orator, his genius was to prefer, to these more public modes of the pulpit and the rostrum, a private tone more suited to the seclusion of an intimate space. From this space he addresses his invisible listener:

> This hour I tell things in confidence,
> I might not tell everybody but I will tell you.
>> "Song of Myself" [LG 1855, lines 386–87; p. 676]

The poet's unseen confidant becomes one of an elect group, a group capable of infinite growth as confidant after confidant is drawn to the poet. After an epic extension of self in various human sympathies ("I am the man, I suffered, I was there"), the poet of "Song of Myself" has proved himself worthy to teach others, and his tone becomes that of a teacher addressing a corps of *élèves*, pupils male and female:

> Eleves I salute you,
> I see the approach of your numberless gangs. . . . I see you
>> understand yourselves and me. . . .
>> [M]y steps drag behind yours yet go before them.
>> I launch all men and women forward with me into
>>> the unknown.
>>> [lines 969–70, 972; p. 697; line 1134; p. 703]

The foreign word "eleves" (in de-accented American form) suggests that this poet-maître differs from other teachers his future pupils may have encountered, that what he bestows is not the schoolmaster's lecture or the philanthropist's public act, but something more private, something closer to a blood transfusion or an infusion of semen:

> Behold I do not give lectures or a little charity,
> What I give I give out of myself.
>> [lines 991–92; p. 698]

If we are for a moment tempted to assimilate this speaker, because of his "behold," to the Jesus of the Gospels, we are brought up short by the violent colloquial intimacy of the lines immediately following, addressed, as if by a drill sergeant, to the weak and imperfect listener-in-futurity:

> You there, impotent, loose in the knees, open your scarfed
>   chops till I blow grit within you,
> Spread your palms and lift the flaps of your pockets.
>
> [line 993; p. 698]

Such a passage reveals the length to which Whitman will go to attach bodily materiality to his unseen future auditors. Nor are his means of conveying materiality always drawn, like these chops and palms, from human appearance. Drawing on his past as a carpenter, Whitman turns his future companion and himself into two lengths of wood in order to render in material terms his wish for identity: "[I] would fetch you whoever you are flush with myself " [line 1081; p. 701]. Given the flexibility of that "myself," the "flush" position of the reader-listener must be continually readjusted.

We have seen Whitman move from a real beloved to an invisible one; from an indifferent contemporary audience to disciples to come; from an absence of pupils in the present to "eleves" as yet unborn. In each case, the poet assumes the literary burden of giving physical reality to the invisible future companion. In the 1855 *Leaves of Grass*, Whitman sometimes confers such reality by making his setting an actual scene (the open road), in which the invitation extended presumes an identification, physical and mental, of one adventurous camerado with another. Two adults, promised to mutual help, and imagined as existing in a common present, are to set off on the open road to see the world and reach God:

Our rendezvous is fitly appointed. . . . God will be there and
wait till we come.

. . . .

My left hand hooks you round the waist,
My right hand points to landscapes of continents, and a plain
public road.

. . . .

Shoulder your duds,[3] and I will mine, and let us hasten forth;
Wonderful cities and free nations we shall fetch as we go.

If you tire, give me both burdens, and rest the chuff of your
hand on my hip,
And in due time you shall repay the same service to me;
For after we start we never lie by again.

[lines 1197, 1212–1216; p. 705]

The marks of physical mutuality here—the bodily contact, the reciprocity of physical gestures given and received, the "duds," and the
promise of first-person-plural perpetuity on the open road—
appear throughout "Song of Myself," as does the fiction of one person confiding in another. At the end of the poem, the departing
poet several times calls out with anxiety, asking for a reciprocal
speech of confidence from the invisible other:

Listener up there! Here you! What have you to confide
to me?

. . . .

Talk honestly, for no one else hears you, and I stay only a
minute longer.

. . . .

Who wishes to walk with me?

Will you speak before I am gone? Will you prove already
    too late?

[lines 1310, 1312, 1319–20; p. 709]

The reassurance implicit in intimate talk between friends or lovers
is one of the seductive appeals of the envisioned mutuality in "Song
of Myself." And although Whitman addresses a "Listener up there,"
that vertically situated listener may be either invisible to the poet in
the present or waiting for the poet in the future.

    After the departure into air of the superbly imagined speaker
at the end of "Song of Myself," the promised intimacy of mutual
talk must vanish, too. The poet becomes part of his native soil as
his body returns to the American version—"dirt"—of the Adamic
dust from which he came. The former intimacy of physical touch is
reproduced in the contact of bootsoles to dirt:

I bequeath myself to the dirt to grow from the grass I love,
If you want me again look for me under your bootsoles.

[lines 1329–30; p. 710]

Dissatisfied with an intimacy that is barred from actual touch by a
membrane of shoe-leather, Whitman imagines himself growing
from the grass to become his future reader's very flesh, transubtan-
tiated from grass into his meat and drink:

You will hardly know who I am or what I mean,
But I shall be good health to you nevertheless,
And filter and fibre your blood.

[lines 1331–33; p. 710]

This extraordinary promise mimics the intimacy of the Eucharist,
in which the Divine Spirit creeps by way of physical nourishment
into the heart's blood.[4] And if his reader-to-be has not yet found
the poet, he must imitate the Christian pilgrim, and search out his

invisible Friend. Whitman closes "Song of Myself" with one last promise, not unlike the promises of Jesus to his disciples before his ascent into heaven:

> Failing to fetch me at first keep encouraged,
> Missing me one place search another,
> I stop some where waiting for you.[5]
>
> [lines 1334–36; p. 710]

Whitman, who had long been waiting in loneliness for an actual camerado to find him on this earth, now, reversing roles, places himself on the road ahead of the camerado of the future, waiting for the listener to seek him out and catch up to him. As he had said earlier in "Song of Myself," "My steps drag behind yours yet go before them" [line 972; p. 697].

Whitman's most original search for a possible grammar of intimacy with the invisible human beings of the future is pursued in the great poem now called by its 1871 name, "The Sleepers." Originally the fourth poem of the untitled twelve of the 1855 *Leaves of Grass*, it was named "Night Poem" in 1856 and "Sleep-Chasings"—its most accurate title—in 1860. "The Sleepers" is the name of its matter, "Sleep-Chasings" the name of its manner. Whitman recites here the many dreams of invisible intimacy that had occurred to him during the years of the "long foreground" (as Emerson's first letter to Whitman called it) to *Leaves of Grass*. "The Sleepers" is constituted by the fantasy of sleeping and dreaming in the company of all the selves of the earth—a materializing of the poet's gift of insight into the lives of others. The sleepers are unaware of the poet's presence as he enters their very beds:

> I go from bedside to bedside. . . . I sleep close with the other
> sleepers, each in turn,

I dream in my dream all the dreams of the other dreamers,
And I become the other dreamers.
"The Sleepers" [*LG* 1855, lines 29–31; p. 724]

However great the imagined intimacy may be of this stealthy in-
sinuation of self into the dreams of others, such unconscious commerce can offer no mutuality or reciprocity; and so, in a further
fantasy, Whitman invents a mobile crowd of metaphysical aerial
companions, very much awake, with whom he can disport himself.
These "nimble ghosts" play hide and seek with him ("cache and
cache again" from the French name for hide and seek, *cache-cache*) in
three elemental realms—ground, sea and air. His *genii loci* are hid-
den from normal perception, but not from the poet: "from me . . .
they [can] hide nothing, and would not if they could." His intimacy
with them is mutual, and is one of playful status-exchange; he is
their "boss," he says, but they make him their "pet" besides, as they
in turn assume authority over him. These equivocal spirits run ahead
of him, lifting their "cunning covers" for him and him alone in a gesture of sexual intimacy:

Well do they do their jobs, those journeymen divine,
Only from me can they hide nothing and would not if
they could.
I reckon I am their boss, and they make me a pet besides,
And surround me, and lead me and run ahead when
I walk,
And lift their cunning covers and signify me with stretched
arms, and resume the way;
Onward we move, a gay gang of blackguards with
mirthshouting music and wild-flapping pennants of joy.
[*LG* 1855, lines 36–41; 724–25][6]

CHAPTER TWO

In this extraordinary moment of exultation, we see a group intimacy achievable only with a "gang" of celestial playmates, male Muses. This mutuality is plural rather than dyadic, and includes not only varied role playing (being a boss at the same time as a pet) but also the gaiety of hide and seek, and the joy of outlawry and music.

Within "The Sleepers," the fantastic parade in the sky cannot last, any more than can the invasion of the beds of sleeping others. Leaving behind that group-intimacy with imaginary companions, as he has left behind the hope of a real lover, the poet concedes that in the end the dark of imagination is a better lover than a spirit or an ordinary man. Whitman takes on the mask of a woman in order to express dissatisfaction with physical intercourse with a male lover; the woman turns away from her human partner to make darkness itself into her lover:

> Darkness you are gentler than my lover—his flesh was sweaty
>   and panting,
> I feel the hot moisture yet that he left me.
>
> [lines 51–54; p. 725]

The poet's sleep-chasings come to an end with no male lover in sight at all, singular or plural, real or invisible, present or future. The speaker, now solitary, finds the darkness to be not a lover or camerado but rather his mother, as the erotic is sublimated and obliterated in the regression to the nocturnal womb, the prenatal scene of an intimacy entirely symbiotic, never to be replicated. At the close of "The Sleepers," the invisible listener is Sleep, the all-embracing mother, guaranteeing for the prophetic speaker a dawn rebirth:

> I will duly pass the day O my mother and duly return to
>   you; . . .
> Not the womb yields the babe in its time more surely than I
>   shall be yielded from you in my time.
>
> [lines 202, 204; p. 731]

42

In "The Sleepers," Whitman is still comparing the intimacy with actual human beings that he seeks (and has occasionally found, as we could see from the passage on the "first sweet eating and drinking") with imagined intimacies of various sorts: the plural intimacy with the idyllic "journeymen divine" (who never again return in Whitman's work); the somber intimacy with the "darkness" that is preferable to the earthly lover; and the primal infantile intimacy with the all-encompassing mother. "The Sleepers," in its gentle voyeurism, is Whitman's ultimate attempt at union with actual living beings in the present, but the attempt is not wholly satisfactory, as the departures into fantasized intimacies with the invisible reveal. And physical mutuality, though it is movingly represented in "The Sleepers," seems not to be available to the speaker himself, who can view its Utopian and reconciliatory form only in others—in Washington embracing his troops, in the poet's mother sitting with the beautiful squaw, in the coupled sleepers. Nowhere in the poem, however, is physical closeness accompanied by sexual intercourse; that potential is rendered impossible by the unconsciousness of the sleepers:

> The sleepers are very beautiful as they lie unclothed . . . ,
> The bare arm of the girl crosses the bare breast of her lover,
>   they press close without lust, his lips press her neck,
> The father holds his grown or ungrown son in his arms with
>   measureless love, and the son holds the father in his
>   arms with measureless love,
> The white hair of the mother shines on the white wrist of the
>   daughter,
> The breath of the boy goes with the breath of the man, friend
>   is inarm'd by friend.
>   [lines 161, 165–68; p. 363]

The central Whitmanian sign of reciprocity, the repetition of identical words to show body adjoined to body, is openly in evidence here: "bare . . . bare," "press / . . . press," "holds . . . / holds," "in his arms . . . / in his arms," "with measureless / love . . . with measureless love," "white . . . white," "breath . . . breath," "friend . . . / friend." Not one of these coupled human beings is intimately available to the solitary poet, who, in the poem's final line, can find in the night only a single hearer, his invisible mother: "I will duly pass the day O my mother, and duly return to you."

"The Sleepers" is Whitman's great yearning poem of the desire for intimacy and reciprocity in actual physical life. It is only by relinquishing this present desire, at least temporarily, that he is enabled to write his greatest poem of intimacy with the invisible companion-in-futurity—the 1856 "Crossing Brooklyn Ferry," originally called "Sun-Down Poem" [pp. 135–40]. In it, Whitman confronts the difficulties intrinsic to the creation of a physical materialization of the invisible. Whereas George Herbert contented himself with tonalities of intimacy stemming from emotional desire, and did not—indeed, could not—concern himself with depiction of the body of the invisible Being with whom he entered into relation, Whitman—insisting that the body *is* the soul—had to confer on the listener in futurity a real body carrying out real actions. The living sleepers—unconscious—could be arranged, by Whitman, in the desired positions of mutual embrace, embraces for which Whitman ached. But those immobile sleepers could not be made to carry out any real actions, and could not therefore become imagined physical companions for the poet himself. In a tremendous leap of imagination, seeking for future physical embodiments of himself, Whitman takes as his surrogates the ceaseless crowds of persons who will, in their day, take the Brooklyn Ferry, as he is doing at the present sundown moment. He projects the crowds into a future space and time made credible, firm, and indubitable because it is scheduled by the beatifically certain routines of the crowded ferry itself and by the atmospherically ordained daily setting of the sun. If

Whitman himself on the Brooklyn Ferry is real, so, then, will be the invisible, but predictable, sundown passengers of the future.

"Crossing Brooklyn Ferry" allows its several marvelously scored intimacies of address to cohere and dissolve without authorial prefiguration. The second-person addressee of the overture (strophe 1) is not a person but an environment: "Flood-tide below me! I see you face to face! / Clouds of the west—sun there half an hour high—I see you also face to face." Then, by the slip of a single sound, the "clouds" become "crowds," the new generalized target of address: these crowds are those now surrounding Whitman on the ferry: "Crowds of men and women attired in the usual costumes, how curious you are to me!" Without any break, the crowds become identical ones of the future: "I am with you, you men and women of a generation, or ever so many generations hence." It is at this point that Whitman begins to constitute—with tautologically repeated verbs in the parallel pattern "Just as you, so I"—the physical being of his future ferry-passengers. Emphasizing that he himself "many and many a time cross'd the river," he guarantees, by the iteration of his own action, the iterability of the same action in the future.

Whitman's most ingenious method of bringing his future surrogates into sensuous existence is to represent the future by their present tense, and his own current present by a continuous past, as he turns himself into their past precursor. *He* crossed the river long ago, "of old," he says, but his surrogates are crossing it *now*: it is *their* actions that are present, vivid, visible, and immediate:

> Just as you feel when you look on the river and sky, so I felt,
> Just as any of you is one of a living crowd, I was one of a
>   crowd,
> Just as you are refresh'd by the gladness of the river and the
>   bright flow, I was refresh'd.

This pattern in "Just as you . . . so I" making the future the present, is replaced by the repeated "I too," which governs the neutral verbs "saw" and "look'd," maintained throughout the rest of strophe 3. Against that optic constant, all the objects looked on and seen become the variables, as the eye takes in elements of the air, the water, and the landscape—sunlight, ships, foundry chimneys. Among all these sights one is particularly striking: "I too," says the poet, in a dazzling line, "Look'd at the fine centrifugal spokes of light round the shape of my head in the sunlit water." This natural halo, appropriating traditional iconographical representations of the sun or rays within the aureole of a deity, is composed of spokes of light streaming out centrifugally from the poet's own head, as though they are thoughts issuing from his brain made visible by their reflection in the water. This transfiguring image attests to the degree to which "Crossing Brooklyn Ferry" is a poem celebrating, without equivocation, the divinity of man.

Whitman continues, in the fourth strophe, to insist on the perfect equation of himself and his counterparts in the future, but he leaves behind the "you" of direct address in order to move to a more philosophical plane, referring now to the ferry-passengers-to-come in the third person, as "others" (as he had done in his second strophe), placing them at a distance from his immediate companions in the actual present crossing:

> The men and women I saw were all near to me,
> Others the same—others who look back on me because I
>   look'd forward to them,
> (The time will come, though I stop here to-day and to-night.)

With that completed declaration of a wonderful mutuality spanning time and space, joining the poet to those "who look back on me because I look'd forward to them," Whitman surges forward, returning to his former form of direct address, "I too," this time

emphasizing to his listeners—though speaking posthumously—
his own temporal and existential reality, both mental and physical:

> I too lived, Brooklyn of ample hills was mine. . . .
> I too felt the curious abrupt questionings stir within me. . . .
> I too had receiv'd identity by my body.

The proudly quiet claims of this are succeeded by a self-epitaph,
more philosophically complete, in which the poet is shown, when
alive, to have been consciously aware of the body's foundational role
in his individual being, and its equally important role in the subsequent unfolding of his life:

> That I was I knew was of my body, and what I should be I
>   knew I should be of my body.

The "you" to whom Whitman's comforting "I too" is now directed
has narrowed to a singular rather than a plural addressee, and is set
with Whitman among "the rest" of his fellow-humans:

> It is not upon you alone the dark patches fall,
> The dark threw its patches down upon me also. . . .
> Nor is it you alone who know what it is to be evil,
> I am he who knew what it was to be evil. . . .
> Lived the same life with the rest, the same old laughing,
>   gnawing, sleeping.

Whitman is still separating himself from his future listener by using
distinct tenses for the two persons in the couple: "you know . . . I
knew." Slowly, however, in the seventh strophe, Whitman and his
imagined replacement on the ferry begin to inhabit the same tense, to
experience the invisible mood felt during true intimacy. The distinc-
tion of tenses is maintained at first: "you have . . . I had." But with a
query, the poet and his listener come conjecturally face to face in an
indeterminate present-tense lyric "now":

> Who knows, for all the distance, but I am as good as looking
>   at you now, for all that you cannot see me?

The present-tense looking becomes Whitman's quasisexual transfusion of self, reciprocated by his addressee, who looks even if he
cannot see. The human mystery of mutual (sexual) recognition is
analogized to the transformative fluidity of language in transmit-
ting meaning:

> What is more subtle than this which ties me to the woman or
>   man that looks in my face?
> Which fuses me into you now, and pours my meaning into
>   you?

This fantasy occasions the moment of greatest intimacy in "Crossing Brooklyn Ferry," when, at last, the poet can use that first-person
plural on which he had so joyously rung changes in "We Two": "We
understand then do we not?" In his subsequent exultant addresses
to the sea and the light, the poet's halo is distributed to all and any
who follow him on the ferry:

> Receive the summer sky, you water, and faithfully hold it till
>   all downcast eyes have time to take it from you!
> Diverge, fine spokes of light, from the shape of my head, or
>   any one's head, in the sunlit water!

For elegiac truthfulness, Whitman must relinquish the ultimate fantasy of an invisible camerado who—following the tem-
plate set down by the poet—performs in the future bodily actions
identical to the poet's own. In the metaphysical but ascetic coda to
"Crossing Brooklyn Ferry," as in the overture, the plural "you" who
are addressed are not persons but aspects of the physical world.
Whitman's mental companions are no longer, as they were in "The
Sleepers," spirits gamboling in the sky. Rather, they are the silent

material phenomena of his environment, the objects of sense-recognition. These constitute the "necessary film" that envelops the soul; they are the only means through which the soul can be known. The phenomena absorbed by the senses cannot forsake the poet, will never be unfaithful, are not items in a fantasy; they endure as the patient and undemanding support of all the poet's words. Whitman addresses them with the intimate tone of a lover:

> You have waited, you always wait, you dumb, beautiful
>   ministers,
> We receive you with free sense at last, and are insatiate
>   henceforward. . . .
> We fathom you not—we love you—there is perfection in
>   you also,
> You furnish your parts toward eternity,
> Great or small, you furnish your parts toward the soul.

In this praise of the earth's profferings, we unexpectedly encounter the word "eternity." It makes us realize that it is only in an eternity imagined as ever-present and always available that Whitman's intimate "we" can include both himself and his invisible fellow-passengers to come. Brave as the poet has been in conceiving the desired companion of the future as a physical being whose actions reiterate the poet's own, he can end "Crossing Brooklyn Ferry" only outside human companionship, solitary among the earth's beautiful but silent appearances.

By 1860, Whitman knows, as he intimates in "Facing West from California's Shores," that were he to search the whole world through, he would not find the human mutuality he sought, though it has been the very motive of his quest:

> Round the earth having wander'd,
> Now I face home again, very pleas'd and joyous,

(But where is what I started for so long ago?
And why is it yet unfound?)
        "Facing West from California's Shores" [p. 95]

Balked of human company, Whitman feels—as in the close of "The Sleepers"—drawn toward an intimacy with Death. His leaves of grass have become, in "Scented Herbage of My Breast," perennial "tomb leaves." The poet at first displaces his attraction to Death into an address to his own poems and their mysterious buried roots, but his attention insensibly drifts toward Death itself:

> You are often more bitter than I can bear, you burn and
>   sting me,
> Yet you are beautiful to me you faint tinged roots, you make
>   me think of death,
> Death is beautiful from you (what indeed is finally beautiful
>   except death and love?)
> O I think it is not for life I am chanting here my chant of
>   lovers, I think it must be for death. . . .
> (I am not sure but the high soul of lovers welcomes death
>   most,)
> Indeed O death, I think now these leaves mean precisely the
>   same as you mean. . . .
> Give me your tone therefore O death, that I may accord with it.
>   "Scented Herbage of My Breast" [p. 98]

How does a living poet come to conceive Death fully enough to be able to address it with such intimacy of tone, to make it one of his invisible listeners? Whitman begins by assimilating Death to companions already loved, those "beautiful, dumb, ministers" of the earth, the phenomena that constitute his knowledge of life and of himself. Because they are earthly beings, their nature presupposes its own necessary dissolution. Knowing them, then, he already knows Death, knows it sufficiently well to address it as the "real reality":

> . . . You hide in these shifting forms of life, for reasons, and . . .
> they are mainly for you,
> . . . [Y]ou beyond them come forth to remain, the real reality,
> . . . [B]ehind the mask of materials you patiently wait, no
> matter how long,
> . . . [Y]ou will one day perhaps take control of all,
> . . . [Y]ou will perhaps dissipate this entire show of
> appearance.
>
> [p. 99]

Whitman's notions of evolutionary progress have reversed themselves here as they foresee devolution toward entropy, in which death undoes all forms, all appearances. Still addressing Death, the poet concedes his whole universe to extinction, to the evacuation of meaning, as Death stretches out to absorb all time, as far as he can see:

> . . . [M]ay-be you are what it is all for, but it does not last so
> very long,
> But you will last very long.
>
> [p. 99]

Within Whitman's prewar poetry, the primal wish for human intimacy, whether with the visible or the invisible, strives continually against a deathwards drift toward intimacy with nonbeing. Whereas in the poem "Of the Terrible Doubt of Appearances" the poet declares that all doubts about appearance and reality "are curiously answer'd by my lovers, my dear friends, . . . / He ahold of my hand has completely satisfied me" [p. 103], this faith in the erotic idyll is countered, he admits, in every man by "the sick, sick dread lest the one he lov'd might secretly be indifferent to him" ["Recorders Ages

Hence," p. 104]. The terrible doubt of appearances can now under-mine even the fantasy of the surrogate-in-futurity. Asking in his title, "Are you the New Person Drawn toward Me?" Whitman warns the potential listener away, adding, "Have you no thought O dreamer that it may be all maya, illusion?" [pp. 105–6] The Manhattan that produces no satisfactory lover can seem at such moments a hateful and hostile city, even if in the Utopian dream following on such fear the poet sees a different city, one "invincible to the attacks of the whole of the rest of the earth, / . . . the new city of Friends" [p. 113]. The frustrating fluctuations of actual erotic life erase both the "shuddering longing ache of contact" [p. 113] and its Utopian urban prolongation, and Whitman the lover declines into Whitman the messianic leader, deprecating his own "arguments, similes, rhymes," and promising instead "the progress of souls":

> Whoever denies me it shall not trouble me,
> Whoever accepts me he or she shall be blessed and shall bless
> me. . . .
> (I and mine do not convince by arguments, similes, rhymes,
> We convince by our presence.) . . .
>
> Allons! to that which is endless as it was beginningless. . . .
> All parts away for the progress of souls.
>
> "Song of the Open Road"
> [lines 67–68, 138–39, 166–67; p. 181]

When the appalling griefs of the Civil War suddenly de-manded representation, Whitman's plural imagined intimacies of 1855, 1856, and 1860—the intimacy with the lover, with the hoped-for friend-camerado, with the sleepers and the ghosts, with the invisible ferry-passengers in futurity, with the "dumb, beautiful, ministers," and with obliterating Death—were shocked into sus-pension. Deaths of soldiers on the battlefields or in the hospitals began to supersede for Whitman his own fantasized futures. Tones of intimacy do not of course lapse altogether, but they become discouraged: he apologizes to his camerado for not having "the least idea what is our destination / Or whether we shall be victorious, or utterly quell'd and defeated" ["As I Lay with My Head in Your Lap Camerado," p. 271]. New forms of intimate discourse inevitably arise for Whitman in the context of war, as in "Vigil Strange I Kept on the Field One Night." But such a poem has recourse to the conventional address of elegy, already codified by generations of lament. The solitary communion of the poet with Death is compelled to widen into collective elegy in the "carol" sung at the end of "When Lilacs Last in the Dooryard Bloom'd"—an address to Death voiced not in dyadic intimacy, as in "The Sleepers," but in the presence of "the debris and debris of all the slain soldiers of the war" [p. 283].

After the war, much in Whitman becomes retrospective, as he reflects on himself as a recorder of his era and mediator of its voices. We see him in 1880, presenting to us the pictures in his brain, at first addressing us in the impersonal tones of the "cicerone" of his cranial "picture gallery"; he is the interpreter, to his invisible listeners in the future, not only of the memories stored in his mind but also of himself as their expositor:

> In a little house keep I pictures suspended, it is not a fix'd
>   house,
> It is round, it is only a few inches from one side to the other;
> Yet behold, it has room for all the shows of the world, all
>   memories!
> Here the tableaus of life, and here the groupings of death;
> Here, do you know this? this is cicerone himself,
> With finger rais'd he points to the prodigal pictures.
>   "My Picture Gallery" [p. 338]

The physical materiality of Whitman's verse-self is present to the last, not only in the phrenological view of the human head ("round," "a few inches from one side to the other") but also in the unforeseen appearance of that staple of European museums, the cicerone, who serves as Whitman's third-person surrogate, materialized by means of his bodily gesture, his pointing finger. The sudden buttonholing intimacy of Whitman's second address to the imagined viewer— "Here, do you know this?"—brings us into a present that is simultaneous with that of the cicerone instructing us, while the prodigal groups of pictures, contemporaneous with the poet who made them, recede into the presented past of a museum. The relation of cicerone to tourist-spectator is, however, hardly an intimate one. And Whitman's later longings for a camerado are wistful rather than urgent, as in the 1871 "Passage to India," where the soul finds God and "the aim attain'd, / As fill'd with friendship, love complete, the Elder Brother found, / The Younger melts in fondness in his arms" [p. 352]. Elder and Younger Brother have no need for language in this posthumous embrace: words have no commerce with this silent sibling intimacy. And although at the close of "Passage to India" Whitman turns, as he did at the end of "Crossing Brooklyn Ferry," to address elements of the universe, the objects in view are far distant ("O sun and moon and all you stars!" [p. 353]), and intimacy of language is lost.

In the end, when the aging and ill poet fears he has exhausted his store of expression, he imagines that his ardent words have disintegrated into their atoms, the separate letters of metal type of which they were composed. As Whitman the erstwhile printer, three years before his death, looks at a font of type, he senses within the "pallid slivers" of lead a host of future "unlaunched voices" ready to erupt in wrath or argument, praise, leer, or prayer. But besides supplying matter, the font of type—Whitman the poet reminds us—can generate manner. Not only single words but also oceanic Whitmanian lines, by turns tumultuous and serene, slumber as yet unawakened within the type. "A Font of Type," although it does not, as in the old manner, produce a poet of the future and address him, is, despite its verbless syntax of exhibition, a poem of alchemical power, in which the printer's leaden font-names—nonpareil, brevier, bourgeois, long primer—are mined for, and transformed into, the gold of passionate voices:

> This latent mine—these unlaunch'd voices—passionate
>> powers,
> Wrath, argument, or praise, or comic leer, or prayer devout,
> (Not nonpareil, brevier, bourgeois, long primer merely,)
> These ocean waves arousable to fury and to death,
> Or sooth'd to ease and sheeny sun and sleep,
> Within the pallid slivers slumbering.
>
> [p. 427]

Whitman is still, even at Death's door, the poet of futurity, pointing out, as cicerone of the print shop, the voicings of human address—of wrath or argument, praise or prayer—that slumber in the cases of the temporarily distributed type, until they are awakened by a creative human hand assembling the type into words and lines. Those voicings slumber in him, too, still pressing his poetic powers to join letter to letter and launch his soul into those speech-acts that the type-letters exist to embody; yet in the weakness of his last years Whitman has no longer the energy to write the poems latent in the type, and the poem becomes an implicit elegy for his poetic self.

In the poem placed last in the 1891 "Deathbed Edition" of *Leaves of Grass* we encounter—as we might expect—an intimate address to an invisible listener, but this address is directed neither to a future surrogate nor to Death. Addressing his own imagination, his "Fancy," Whitman adopts the classical elegiac *Ave atque Vale*—"Hail and

Farewell"—but characteristically reverses it to an optimistic "Farewell and Hail," with the English "Farewell" Americanized into "Good-bye." Although the poem allows reminiscence, it still ends with a look to the future—"Good-bye—and hail! my Fancy" [p. 468]. W. B. Yeats wrote in a late letter that the last kiss is given to the void. But for Whitman, the last kiss is given to the future. By so powerfully imagining futurity into physical being—in ferry-passengers, in a font of type, in an immortal Fancy—Whitman created an intimacy of address to invisible listeners that staunchly engaged their materiality as much as his spiritual union with them, bringing to lyric intimacy new tonalities, eroticized and future-oriented.

If we construct the ethical atmosphere of an actual social world from Whitman's fantasized one, we would find it a world that ratifies and values all forms of attachment, whether of lover to lover, teacher to pupil, or wound-dresser to the wounded. The projective imagination modeled for us by the poet would be, if we practiced it, a means to social tolerance and empathetic cohesion. It is sometimes hard to remember—such is the intimacy of Whitman's tone—that in most of his poems he had no visible addressee. His effusions and transfusions and perfusions are so convincing on the page that we forget that they had to stream outward into the unknown, like those spokes of light around his illuminated face, like those filaments launched into its "vacant vast surrounding" by his noiseless patient spider. If his lyrics of social imagination move us as they address us—his invisible listeners of the future—it is because he so clearly saw the ethics of intimacy as it ought to be and, in his speculative and democratic imagination, already was.

THREE

John Ashbery and the Artist
of the Past

As we have seen, many lyric speakers have addressed, in intimate terms, an invisible listener. In the work of George Herbert, the invisible listener is God; in Whitman, it is often a listener-in-futurity. Ashbery is one of those—John Berryman is another—who have sought intimacy with a listener from the past: Anne Bradstreet for Berryman, Francesco Parmigianino for Ashbery. And Ashbery, like Whitman, envisages a second invisible listener—his reader, of whom many of his poems are acutely conscious. Ashbery's long ars poetica, *Self-Portrait in a Convex Mirror*, depends intrinsically on the establishing of an intimacy between himself and the long-dead painter whom he addresses. I want to comment here not only on Ashbery's changes of address in *Self-Portrait*, but also on how he allows the ethics of social life to enter the verbal space of lyric.

Because Ashbery has not engaged in explicit political and social action and commentary after the fashion of Allen Ginsberg, Adrienne Rich, W. S. Merwin, or others of his generation, he has sometimes been thought socially apathetic, solipsistic, or narcissistic. In view of this critique—which I believe to be inaccurate—it is ironic that Ashbery's greatest formal contribution has been to bring into lyric a vast social lexicon of both English English and American English—common speech, journalistic cliché, business and technical and scientific language, allusion to pop culture as well as to canonical works. In Ashbery's lines, words are often sprung free of their usual contexts: words that began in vertical relation to each other (as archaic words "stand above" contemporary ones, or formal words "above" slang), or in no relation at all to each other (such as the words "tacked-up" and "angst") are brought into horizontal (metonymic) intimacy with each other, in a slightly surreal, but comprehensible, narration.

For instance, in the case I'm about to quote—from the poem "Grand Galop" (1975)—Ashbery hybridizes two stories—the medieval myth of a knight's archaic journey to a tower where he will suffer an ordeal, and its contemporary parodic equivalent, the journey of the hero of a Western movie into a gully where he discovers himself in one of the dead mining towns of the Gold Rush. Naturally—since Ashbery is symbolizing everyone's life-experience— the quest is unsuccessful. From the point of view of the now-enlightened speaker, looking backward, the story is both true and ironized, absurd and yet angst-ridden. The Ashberian speaker tacitly assumes that his readers have themselves undergone the archetypal well-worn story he is recapitulating, even if he voices it with the impersonal "one":

> One approaches a worn, round stone tower
> Crouching low in the hollow of a gully
> With no door or window but a lot of old license plates
> Tacked up over a slit too narrow for a wrist to pass through
> And a sign: "Van Camp's Pork and Beans."
> From then on in: angst-colored skies, emotional
> withdrawals[.][1]

In his syntax as well as in his diction, Ashbery juxtaposes the high ("One approaches a worn, round stone tower") and the demotic ("From then on in").

Ashbery's history of emotional life invites us to become co-creators of the poem, as we jump, following the poem's lexicon, from *Childe Roland* to John Wayne to medieval illustrations of narrow slits in fortified walls, to Miner's Gulch, to Kierkegaard, to Freud. Ashbery cordially assumes that his range of reference is our own—that any of us who tend to read poetry will find hand- and footholds in this stratified cliff-face of twentieth-century sensibility. The moral result of travelling through such a heterodox lexical atmosphere is to make us subconsciously ask, as we read, to what degree we ourselves subscribe to these culturally available myths of explanation. Do we secretly imagine ourselves as knights embarked on Arthurian quests, or as just plain American folks reducing venerable cultural icons to mundane license plates? As creatures of Kierkegaardian angst, or as perpetrators or victims of Freudian "emotional withdrawals?" Any recognizable fragments of language and imagination are welcome to claim a room in the accepting hostel of the poet's mind. As Ashbery says in "Houseboat Days," "The mind is so hospitable, taking in everything / Like boarders" [*SP*, 231].

Only one constant underlies all this variation, and that, paradoxically, is change. Experiential change—with its ever-accelerating pace—is one of Ashbery's two great moral subjects (love is the other). But how can change be attractively (or at least comically) represented so as to lead us to accept it, even to welcome it, as the basis of an ever-provisional moral life? And how can the lyric—the genre of intimacy—summon into its solitary precinct a sense of our changing society at large, so as to make us, as readers, intimate not only with the author as a private fellow-sufferer but also with his social predicaments (and therefore, by implication, with our own)? Ashbery overcomes the first difficulty by his colloquial charm, inducing us to "live along the line," change by change, with him; he solves the second by his enormous lexical range, which exhibits what he called, writing of Degas, a "Balzacian knowledge of . . . details."[2]

Since the loop of co-creation between Ashbery and his reader is indispensable if the reader is to follow and understand his poetry, Ashbery—more even than Whitman—conceives of lyric as a projected colloquy. There can of course be no actual colloquy—the poet may very well be dead by the time a future reader comes across the poem—but it is the imagined projection of colloquy with an invisible listener that enables the Ashbery poem to be written at all. Ashbery is well aware of how rare it is that any reader gives any poem any attention, and equally aware of the paradox implicit in the poet's creation of a spoken colloquy that cannot take place except with the reader's cooperation. A paradoxical oxymoron—the "I-ness" of you; the "you-ness" of me—subtends the union of those two unlike things, "I" and "you," in the poet's colloquy-projection. In 1981, Ashbery's paradoxes and oxymorons issue in a poignantly modest sixteen-line quasi-sonnet by that name (SP 283) in which the poet acts out, in terms successively playful, ironic, and pleading, his ethics of the intimate lyric, by which "it"—the poem—mediates between the "I" of the poet and the "you" of the reader:

Paradoxes and Oxymorons

This poem is concerned with language on a very plain level.
Look at it talking to you. You look out a window
Or pretend to fidget. You have it but you don't have it.
You miss it, it misses you. You miss each other.

Ashbery does not say "We miss each other." It is not, at first glance, the poet that the reader is to encounter in the poem: the poem, having been conceived, is already an "it," an object with an achieved contour. Yet the poem also manifests, as the heard voice of lyric, an established personal presence: "[The two of] You miss each other," says the poet, comparing the personal poem-presence and its nonreader to two people who have failed to meet. The poem can also—since it is conceived of as a personal presence—feel inner emotion. Here, it feels the pain of a rejected suitor:

> The poem is sad because it wants to be yours, and cannot be.

Disappointed at its failure to arouse the reader, the poem introduces a question that the potential (but as yet evasive) reader might ask. It is implied that the reader, mildly nettled by the schoolmasterish tone of the opening lines, questions the author's conceptual language: "What's a plain level?" The author's answer defends the "plain level," but also insists on the literariness, the intrinsic play, of the art-work:

> What's a plain level? It is that and other things,
> Bringing a system of them into play. Play?
> Well, actually, yes, but I consider play to be
>
> A deeper outside thing, a dreamed role-pattern,
> As in the division of grace these long August days
> Without proof. Open-ended.

The "plain level" and a host of other things (ideas, hopes, learning, rhetorical flourishes, metaphor) come into play and become an Ashberian "system," "a dreamed role-pattern," an imagined holograph-projection of a possible way to live, an "[o]pen-ended" project. The poem hopes to divide its grace with a reader, as sunlight spreads its grace through an August day. It is up to the reader to see whether the "dreamed role-pattern" is a "play" he can enter into. The invitation is extended; but it can offer the reader no proof of value beyond its own attractions.

The author concedes that as the poet's dream condenses into actual language and mechanical transcription, much of it—sometimes all—is lost:

> And before you know it
> It gets lost in the steam and chatter of typewriters.

The experience of today's creation is over, and the poet must begin again tomorrow. What induces the poet to begin over and over? asks Ashbery, and answers that he is motivated by the unconscious and therefore unmet needs of his imagined listener. The poet hopes to introduce the reader to aspects both of himself and of his own era, aspects that he might miss without the poet's intervention. The poet addresses his necessary but fickle potential reader:

> I think you exist only
> To tease me into doing it, on your level, and then you aren't
>   there
> Or have adopted a different attitude.

If the reader has adopted a dissenting or evasive attitude, it means he has already been persuaded into a different role-pattern, one dreamed by someone more powerful than the poet: a more compelling author, an authoritative parent, a convincing political party, an evangelizing church. Ashbery, whose view of life is fundamentally a comic one, avoids this possible unhappy ending, glimpsed in the wings, in which the reader would reject the offered poem. Instead, he gives us a happy ending, in which an angel in the form of the poem bestows on the reader a life-companion who is both the poet and—miraculously—a new version of the reader himself. Having internalized the dreamed role-pattern of the poem, the reader is morally reconstituted. As Ashbery puts it at the close:

> And the poem
> Has set me softly down beside you. The poem is you.

In Ashbery's multiplication of the poet's social role in "Paradoxes and Oxymorons," the poet is the remote author of the written poem, the intimate speaking presence created within it, the invisible winged conveyor of the poem into the imagination of the reader, and the identical twin of the reader who has internalized the poetic role-pattern as his own.

In his most famous poem of colloquy, the *Self-Portrait in a Convex Mirror*, Ashbery casts himself not only as a writer but also as a "reader"—or, because he is here confronting a painting, as a viewer. We learn that in 1959, in the Vienna Kunsthistoriches Museum, in the company of his lover the poet Pierre [Martory], Ashbery came across Francesco Parmigianino's exquisite small round painting called *Self-Portrait in a Convex Mirror* (which Peter Schjeldahl recently described as "art history's most talismanic object before Marcel Duchamp").[3] Standing before the portrait, the young Ashbery received a shock of the sort related in "Paradoxes and Oxymorons": the poem is you, the painting was himself. Unable to forget that intense recognition, and wanting to understand it, Ashbery began to read historical and aesthetic commentary on the painting. More than a decade later, in the 552-line poem of 1972, the poet reconstitutes that original 1959 experience—in which a love-relation, self-recognition, and aesthetic admiration were entwined—and integrates with it the information he has subsequently acquired about the portrait.[4] Ashbery uses the Parmigianino painting, and himself as its spectator, as the model by which to draw his own self-portrait as a twentieth-century poet in intimate colloquy with a dead artist and a contemporary or future reader. A transhistorical wave of response connects the present observer of the painting to all those before him who have been moved by Parmigianino's work, from Pope Clement to the art critic Sydney Freedberg; the group even includes the Germans who invaded Parmigianino's studio during the sack of Rome in 1527, and "amazed at his sang-froid," let him escape. Ashbery sends out a ray of social imagination to Parmigianino's era, and a further ray to the terminology of art criticism from Parmigianino's time to our own (Vasari to Freedberg). In his vulnerable and arresting poem Ashbery enacts the feelings that an

impassioned observer of a painting—or the reader of a poem—
might experience; he passes from detached objectivity to awakened
sympathy, from scholarly interest to aesthetic investment, from self-
referential meditation to an immediate and heartfelt address to the
long-dead painter, only to find himself obliged, in the end, to drop
the attachment he has so deeply formed.

Why was it this portrait in which Ashbery recognized himself
so deeply that more than a decade after seeing it he is still possessed by it, and must reconstitute it in the medium of words, creating his own self-portrait by means of Parmigianino's own? For
Ashbery, the supremely interesting, and deeply confirming, deci-
sion of the painter was the conspicuous and purposeful distortion
of the "reality" that the painting purports to represent—a distortion caused by Parmigianino's startling rejection of an ordinary
flat reflecting mirror in favor of a convex one. In the actual painting, the painter's young and beautiful face, because it is reflected
from the center of the mirror, is affected hardly at all; and the window in the background is neutral enough not to disturb the viewer
by its curvature. What *is* distorted by enlargement, greatly so, is the
right hand of the painter, his creative hand, which extends itself in
the foreground toward the viewer but then curves away. Here is
Ashbery's recreation of his first impression of the painting, beginning casually, as if in conversation with his reader, and already as-
cribing motion and volition to the represented hand of the painter:

> As Parmigianino did it, the right hand
> Bigger than the head, thrust at the viewer
> And swerving easily away, as though to protect
> What it advertises. A few leaded panes, old beams,
> Fur, pleated muslin, a coral ring run together
> In a movement supporting the face, which swims
> Toward and away like the hand

Except that it is in repose. It is what is
Sequestered.

In the rest of the poem, Ashbery veers between seeing the
portrait-face (and its soul) as a thing sequestered in an artifact and
treating it as a person available for colloquy—as a detail obeying
the law of its construction and as a presence speaking to its viewer.
We can understand better Ashbery's notion of the ineluctable se-
questration of any individual's soul if we read his interpretation of
a drawing by Saul Steinberg entitled "Gabinetto del Proprio Niente,"
which represents an alchemist's chamber exhibiting wittily reveal-
ing personal contents, but containing no human figure. In *Reported
Sightings*, Ashbery comments on this uninhabited room, the fin-
ished symbol of consciousness:

> This last is from one of Steinberg's most moving drawings, and
> perhaps epitomizes his strange, comfortably uncomfortable
> world. Life is a room, empty except for the furniture (no person
> can enter it because it is already inside us). The furniture is
> both useful and ornamental, but none of it will be used because
> no one will ever descend the steps marked with the days of the
> week or enter through the open door, beyond which one glimpses
> a tree whose trunk and branches are marked with inscriptions,
> too far away, alas, to be readable. Yet it all does have a function,
> that of a symbol, the only function we need concern ourselves
> with, since it includes everything by telling about it. The act of
> storytelling alone is of any consequence; what is said gets said
> anyway, and manner is the only possible conjugation of matter.
> "Saul Steinberg" (1970) [*RS*, 284]

In Steinberg's symbol of the impregnable but open consciousness,
one glimpses nature, but not the nature from which the Romantic
poets could read truth; there are inscriptions on the Steinbergian

tree, but (like the Steinbergian passports of our immigrant ancestors) they have become unintelligible. Nonetheless, the alchemical room, in its furniture and structure, gives us enough, symbolically, with which to conjecture the world of the alchemist.

So with the Parmigianino portrait, with its greeting and shielding frontal hand. The contemporary artist goes to the masterpieces of the past seeking an intimate presentness of instruction, colloquy, sympathy. Ashbery does not treat "tradition" as something handed down; rather "tradition" is a source urgently yearned toward by the present. Yet the present-day artist must resist the temptation to slide into inert imitation of its irresistible attractions lest he abandon his own distinctness. Addressing Francesco Parmigianino intimately, by his first name, at the end of the poem, the poet at first asks merely for the withdrawal of the hand that had so touched him, but then realizes that if he is to preserve his own selfhood, he will have to murder what has awakened him:

> Therefore I beseech you, withdraw that hand,
> Offer it no longer as shield or greeting,
> The shield of a greeting, Francesco:
> There is room for one bullet in the chamber:
> Our looking through the wrong end
> Of the telescope as you fall back at a speed
> Faster than that of light to flatten ultimately
> Among the features of the room.

As "the diagram still sketched on the wind" begins to fade, as the illusionistic afterglow of shared aesthetic aim and moral sympathy subsides, the poem, with a Keatsian turn, ends in an embalmed chill, redeemed only by a moment of Proustian memory:

> The hand holds no chalk
> And each part of the whole falls off

And cannot know it knew, except
Here and there, in cold pockets
Of remembrance, whispers out of time.

By recording the powerful modification of his sensibility from
1959 to 1972 by the Parmigianino portrait, Ashbery has drawn his
own self-portrait (but one "distorted" not only by his compression
of thirteen years—and much reading—into a few pages, but also
by his exclusion of other aspects of his life during those years).
Parmigianino's painting has confirmed the young poet's conviction
of the necessity and beauty of aesthetic distortion; it has also fos-
tered the solacing illusion of direct communication between a dead
artist and a living viewer, so much so as to compel the American
beholder to think of the artist not as the dead art-historical "Parmigianino" but as a kindred spirit, the "Francesco" who forsook mimetic
realism—in the crucial presentation of his own body in a self-
portrait—for a candid acknowledgment of the distorting optics of
every enabling aesthetic. Ashbery, as a fellow creator, feels admiration for the distorting power of the distorted hand, as it transcribes
through the medium of paint what the eye registers from the light-
empowered and deliberately chosen convex mirror.

If, as Ashbery declares, every aesthetic representation is skewed
away from transcriptive realism by its own formal law, *and* by historical circumstance, *and* by individual psychology, no direct ethical
injunction to life-action can be deduced from the apparent intimacy with the past that a symbolic object seems to create. We may
think we know Parmigianino's face, but it is itself put into question
through its relation to the disproportionately enlarged hand. Although Ashbery is interested in the epistemological question raised
by the convex mirror and the magnified and ambiguously curving
hand, he is more interested in the ethical question of the company
provided by an artwork. If—as he is convinced—nobody can in

truth enter its alchemical chamber, what is the solace, what is the company, what is the release that we feel when we have encountered and responded to a moving and beautiful work of the past? This is a way of asking what the lyric tradition contributes to our moral life.

In choosing a self-portrait as his vehicle, Ashbery is in part defending his own genre, the intimate lyric. Ashbery does not choose as his symbol the sort of artwork—a history painting or a religious fresco—that would be undergirded by a social or political network of meaning. A self-portrait cannot be said to "mean" anything in the way "The Raft of the Medusa" or a painting of Saint Jerome does. Nor does Parmigianino's work suggest a moral problem by exemplifying an identifiable autobiographical incident, in the manner of Van Gogh's self-portrait with a bandaged ear. The youth reflected in the convex mirror displays no attributes (such as priestly clothing or a scholarly book or a merchant's scales) by which he could be identified or his occupation recognized. He offers us nothing but his questioning gaze, and the subjection of his painting hand to convex distortion. For a moment, in a remarkable exchange of selves, Ashbery becomes the Renaissance youth who has been "englobed" in the portrait, and who longs, in "human" rebellion, to find an exit from the eternizing artifact. In vain: the law of circular form forbids an escape from the chamber of art into actual physical intimacy with others:

> One would like to stick one's hand
> Out of the globe, but its dimension,
> What carries it, will not allow it.
> No doubt it is this, not the reflex
> To hide something, which makes the hand loom large
> As it retreats slightly. There is no way
> To build it flat like a section of wall:

It must join the segment of a circle,
Roving back to the body of which it seems
So unlikely a part, to fence in and shore up the face
On which the effort of this condition reads
Like a pinpoint of a smile, a spark
Or star one is not sure of having seen
As darkness resumes.

Because of the law of aesthetic fulfillment that it must follow—"It must join the segment of a circle. . . . to fence in and shore up the face"—art can offer nothing but

a perverse light whose
Imperative of subtlety dooms in advance its
Conceit to light up: unimportant but meant.

The creating artist in any medium aims, of course, to produce illumination, but his moral or intellectual intent is necessarily deflected to some degree during the execution, since the law of art, not the artist, is the ultimate master of the evolving work. Art as such has no "interior": it is pure surface, but that surface is the "visible core" of its generating intents, moral and formal:

And just as there are no words for the surface, that is,
No words to say what it really is, that it is not
Superficial but a visible core, then there is
No way out of the problem of pathos vs. experience.

The unbreachable gap between the pathos of the artwork—an aesthetic quality—and the experience that produced it and that it produces—a moral quality—means that there is no straight path from the artwork to life-action. The two—aesthetic impression and moral sympathy—cannot coincide in themselves, though they may find temporary coincidence in the mind of one responding to the artwork.

What is it, then, in Ashbery's view, that we can gain by way of moral experience from an artist's self-portrait? First of all, we are enabled to feel a stability impossible to terrestrial beings ("The whole is stable within / Instability, a globe like ours, resting / On a pedestal of vacuum"). The microcosm of the painted world resembles the macrocosm of our globe, but, since it occupies neither collapsing nor expanding real space nor hurtling real time, it can convey the repose of untroubled intimacy, if only within the vacuum-globe's virtual reality. Ashbery addresses the represented Francesco directly, quoting Sir Philip Sidney ("The poet nothing lieth, for he nothing affirmeth"):

> You will stay on, restive, serene in
> Your gesture which is neither embrace nor warning
> But which holds something of both in pure
> Affirmation that doesn't affirm anything.

When we understand that the young man's mysterious gesture holds something of embrace, and something of warning, we have come close to a declaration of what the seeker may gain—what the young Ashbery in Vienna did gain—by way of the interchange of selves with a past artist through a formally understood artwork. He will feel embraced; he will feel warned. The embrace stands for that immediate fascination so great that it seems a communication through time itself; yet the painting's manifest formal law, its impregnability, exerts simultaneously the warning that life as we know it has been distorted within this communication. When the spectator feels "warned," he becomes angry: the globe-chamber of art, which once seemed so open but now seems almost repellently impermeable, keeps its algorithms securely locked inside:

> Actually
> The skin of the bubble-chamber's as tough as

Reptile eggs; everything gets "programmed" there
In due course: more keeps getting included
Without adding to the sum.

Here, the unsettling language of tough-skinned reptile eggs, the chilly image of the quantum-measuring "bubble-chamber," the impersonal functionality of the computer program, and the incomprehensible paradoxes of the mathematics of infinity are all invoked, and they are uttered in the terse syntax, short clause after short clause, of disillusioned repartee—"Actually," this is the truth of the matter. In this passage, as in "Grand Galop" and throughout Ashbery's poetry, we are asked to take the measure of our own era, a period that generates in our minds countless scientific and mathematical images for experience. Do we feel solipsistically impermeable to others? Do we feel ourselves colliding at random like particles in a bubble-chamber? Do we feel "programmed" by an implacable fate? Do we feel both overwhelmed by life's sum and yet, exhaustingly, infinitely penetrable by still more data-entries? Because Ashbery moves so rapidly, we find various moral, epistemological, and pictorial questions raised within us as we read his images. To realize that those images—and numberless more—are already inside us (since we recognize them as we meet them in the poet's self-portrait) is to accept a revised self-portrait of ourselves and our contexts, a portrait reflecting a far more varied landscape of external social circumstance than we customarily admit to our thoughts or written words.

Although the enchantment of the aesthetic embrace so extends comprehension of a far-off sensibility that one wants to address the artist by the intimate name "Francesco," the repulsion of the warning against engulfment is so shocking that one must use the single bullet in the chamber to execute either the past artist or oneself. To kill "Francesco," to allow him to fall back into the dead past is to eliminate a master so powerful that he would quench one's own originality; to be so seduced by "Francesco" that one merely imitates him would be to kill oneself as an artist.

The moral experience of this strange colloquy is a complex one. We are the grateful discoverers of miraculously living sources in the art of the past; we can speak familiarly to the gifted painter as we receive the "greeting" of his extended hand; yet we must remain wary potential creators of our own modern selves (warned away from servile imitation of the past by the shield of the same hand); and we are necessarily imperfect observers, always likely to exit from an artwork (or any other life-enterprise) by succumbing to a failure of attention: "The balloon pops, the attention / Turns dully away." Ashbery's poem reminds us that we are the heirs not only of past art but also of past intellectuality, voiced here by the citing of scholarly commentary:

> Sydney Freedberg in his
> *Parmigianino* says of it: "Realism in this portrait
> No longer produces an objective truth, but a *bizarria*. . . .
> However its distortion does not create
> A feeling of disharmony!"

Such a passage calls us to mental attention, reminding us that Ashbery's poem is itself a third-order discourse, dependent on earlier second-order art-historical discourses such as those of Vasari and Freedberg, which are themselves dependent on anterior first-order philosophical discussions that have revolved around terms such as "objective truth," "disharmony," "distortion," and "*bizarria*." When a part of our consciousness that has been drifting unattached is once again called to attention—as Ashbery successively brings into rapid play such elements as the visual, the intellectual, the historical, the erotic, the scientific, and the literary—we expand our receptivity so as to comply with the multiple and disjunctive lexical orders of the text, themselves reflective of disparate historical and social orders.

"My guide in these matters," says Ashbery to Francesco, "is your self, / Firm, oblique, accepting everything with the same / Wraith of a smile[.]" When we accept "everything," in imitation of Parmigianino/Ashbery, we call on reservoirs of emotional and moral energies that change us. When Ashbery sums up the effect of art, it is with an analogy to the tales of Hoffmann. What is novel in the painting by Parmigianino, he says, is that by its technique and its originality it becomes to us more intimate than a doppel-gänger, substituting within us itself and its own context for our or-dinary consciousness of self, space, and time:

> What is novel is the extreme care in rendering
> The velleities of the rounded reflecting surface
> (It is the first mirror portrait),
> So that you could be fooled for a moment
> Before you realize the reflection
> Isn't yours. You feel then like one of those
> Hoffmann characters who have been deprived
> Of a reflection, except that the whole of me
> Is seen to be supplanted by the strict
> Otherness of the painter in his
> Other room. We have surprised him
> At work, but no, he has surprised us
> As he works.

As Ashbery presents to the reader his own self-portrait, refracted from Parmigianino's, he hopes that "you could be fooled for a mo-ment / Before you realize the reflection / Isn't yours." You have sur-prised him as he writes about Parmigianino—but no, he has sur-prised you as you look at his poem. You have been taken out of your time, and have been immersed in Ashbery's—only to awake,

as when one looks out,
Startled by a snowfall which even now is
Ending in specks and sparkles of snow.
It happened while you were inside, asleep[.]

This Keatsian awakening to the world makes us notice that life
has been moving on while we were suspended in aesthetic intimacy, lulled by the charm of the seductive Ashberian voice. As the
new chill creeps into the air, Ashbery turns away from his intimacy with the vanishing Francesco, and enters instead into intimate colloquy with his present reader. The embrace of the portrait
cannot last. "This is its negative side," says Ashbery, commenting
on the dissolution of the beautiful effect of the mirror-portrait.
"Its positive side is / Making you notice life and the stresses / That
only seemed to go away[.]" And just as Parmigianino found his
studio invaded by the German soldiers as they sacked Rome, so
"What we need now is this unlikely / Challenger pounding on the
gates of an amazed / Castle" to startle the sensibility into a further
revaluation of its contemporary moment, a refreshed originality of
perception.

Ashbery's poem insists on the instability of all self-held positions, moral or epistemological, since all are "thoughts / That peel
off and fly away at breathless speeds." But it also conveys his second
persistent topic: the force of love, which (within our Platonic her-
itage) is the allegorical representative of eternal stability. When the
poet first saw the portrait, he was with Pierre, his lover, and love
was in the ascendant, but now—although Ashbery continues to
believe in the existence of love and in its value for intensifying and
enhancing what we perceive—it is obscured:

Love once
Tipped the scales but now is shadowed, invisible,
Though mysteriously present, around somewhere.

74

Change, as it glides toward death, is now the more apparent of the two co-principles of Ashberian meditation; but it was love that focused (in 1959) and stands ready to focus (at any moment) one's attention on life with a force that only the apprehension of death can equal. The intense scrutiny motivated by love makes its object a paradigm of the whole world as it has been represented in the refining and assimilating attention of the artist:

> The sample
> One sees is not to be taken as
> Merely that, but as everything as it
> May be imagined outside time—not as a gesture
> But as all, in the refined, assimilable state.

Because the artwork has purified itself of the extraneous (while including all, since even the surrounding heterogeneity, perhaps especially the heterogeneity, has itself assumed interior linguistic and symbolic form), the artist's point of view becomes assimilable by others. Yet we cannot derive any specific principles of moral action from the impressions, however intimately felt, that we receive from the artwork, since those are derived from the artist's projection of life onto the idiosyncratic and symbolic plane of art. If almost insensible changes in our moral sensibility take place over time, we perceive them only in the long run (as it is only in 1972 that Ashbery can transcribe the disseminated reflections and decisions generated in him over thirteen years). For Ashbery, the artwork's union of aesthetic law and the illusion of intimacy, its integration of its symbolic parts into a perceived whole, works a significant ratification of inner selfhood and external possibility—although from it we cannot avoid awaking to the fresh demands of a changed moment.

What is the result of looking at a lyric such as Ashbery's for a reader who believes, with Stevens, that artworks help us to live our lives? Because a poet wants above all to make, in each effort, something unique and irreplaceable, he would not like to have all his works collected together as conveyors of his ethical sense. It is precisely the individual drive of each artwork, capable of "distorting" the original moral urgency of the artist, that makes moral paraphrase so difficult. Ashbery, writing on R. B. Kitaj, says that the graphic artist is "constantly scrutinizing all the chief indicators—poetry, pictures, politics, sex, the attitudes of people he sees, and the auras of situations they bring with them—in an effort to decode the cryptogram of the world" ["R. B. Kitaj," *RS*, 308]. For the poet, who is no less observant than the graphic artist or the novelist, but for whom the social order has to be conveyed in words rather than through painted images, dramatic scenes, or the interaction of characters, poetry is a place for the decoding of the resistant semiotics of the contemporary. As the poet's mental accumulation meets the compelling law of form, it is regularized from unintelligibility into a shape that seems "right." The morality of this act, as Wallace Stevens said, consists in rejecting proposed forms that merely "console / Or sanctify." Forms that "console" or "sanctify" are concessions to a nostalgic sentimentality. Parmigianino—and Ashbery after him—refuses the consoling or sanctifying concession implicitly present in transcriptive mimesis, while nonetheless allowing recognizable figuration and emotional intimacy to play dominant roles in his art.

In praising Chardin, Ashbery once wrote of the "magnificent progress" possible as the artist "help[s] the spirit to take a new step":

> If one takes the down-to-earth as point of departure and neither makes nor wastes any effort in trying to rise to an exalted or splendid level, every effort, every contribution of the artistic

genius goes into transfiguring the manner of execution, changing the language, and helping the spirit to take a new step, thus
constituting magnificent progress.

"Chardin" [*RS*, 47]

Part of the "down-to-earth," for poets, is fostering within the lyric
poem a climate of mutual trust between poet and reader. Ashbery
here stands between his predecessor in the past, the Francesco he
both summons and dismisses, and the fictive reader of his own self-
portrait in verse. He addresses both of his invisible listeners in
tones of intimate comprehension and sympathy. Ashbery's invisible
listeners—"Francesco" in fantasy and ourselves in reality—animate
the poem from private meditation on an artwork into colloquy
with a corresponding other, from the solitude of the lyric chamber
to an imagination twinning us with someone more like us than we
had imagined. Poems constitute their invisible listeners as persons
who understand, who will complete the expressive circuit of thought
and language initiated by an artwork, and who will engage in the
imagined ethical modeling of an ideal mutuality.

At the same time, in *Self-Portrait in a Convex Mirror*, the listeners—Francesco and the reader—are embedded in an Ashberian
"cryptogram" of lexical reference which, once decoded, reveals within
each of its metaphorical phrases—from reptile eggs to program-
ming—the late twentieth-century social order from which Ashbery writes. For Ashbery, one of the dilemmas of that social order
as he encountered it in youth was the quarrel among his painter-
friends between figurative realism and abstract expressionism (corresponding to the quarrel between mimesis and surrealism in
poetry). Parmigianino's touching and fascinating and distorted self-
portrait represented to the uncertain young Ashbery the possibility
of a third, and more congenial, conception: that of art as an activity

which, while preserving recognizable figuration, would openly concede and demonstrate the necessary swerve away from transcriptive mimesis implicit in every fictive creation. The poem in which Ashbery calls out to his brother-artist in the past and to ourselves in the present enables us to view that third conception alive on the poet's wayward and mesmerizing page.

CONCLUSION   Domesticating the Unseen

◉◉ The imagining by lyric poets of invisible listeners—a divine person, a camerado of the future, an artist of the past—suggests that there are life-situations where a visible (if absent) addressee (a friend, a lover, a fellow-poet) is insufficient for the poet's needs. We have seen three such predicaments. For Herbert, no human being could embody the ego-ideal represented by Jesus (or Love); for Whitman, no actual nineteenth-century lover was likely to understand a Utopian future founded on a freedom in same-sex love; for Ashbery, no contemporary artist exemplified so strongly as Parmigianino the necessity to an artwork of both figuration and distortion. Invisible listeners continue to be attractive to contemporary poets. Louise Glück's *The Wild Iris* imagines multiple colloquies with God; the Whitmanian direct address bridging the gap between poet and listener reappears in Jorie Graham's frequent entreaties to the "Friend" reading her poems; and Lucie Brock-Broido's *The Master Letters*—borrowing from Dickinson's enigmatic unsent letters to a man she called "Master"—both address and describe one or more invisible others. It is the hypothetical plane on which such encounters occur that attracts poets: there, one is freer than on a literal plane, freer to imagine, to experiment and to speculate. Of course all poetry takes place on a hypothetical plane, but not all such poetry includes, or is based on, colloquy. Precisely because the ethical can be treated most elementally in a relation-of-two, lyrics of hypothetical colloquy are one ideal staging-place for ethical questions. Although many such addresses in the work of Seamus Heaney are

79

directed toward the personally known dead, the poet also composes colloquies with authors long dead and not known in life—Kavanagh, Joyce. And like Ashbery with Parmigianino, he finds corroboration for his own endeavors in their voices and their example.

In poems radiating out toward an invisible listener, we find a kind of lyric Utopia, in which possible models of human relations are produced, scrutinized, revised, and consolidated. There is room in this genre for aspiration, repentance, envy, resentment, joy, and all the other emotions attending relationship. This genre is distinguished from the lyric of solitary meditation (which also can have a Utopian motivation) by the intensity brought to it in its surge toward an invisible other who becomes the site where urgent questions of guilt, love, hope, and trust can be explored and even resolved. Although "vertical" relationships with an invisible listener (such as those motivating many prayers and odes) have a long history in lyric, the poets I have written about in these chapters conceive "horizontal" relationships even with the divine, insisting on the colloquy with the invisible as the fully human speech of one person with another. These poets are the domesticators of the invisible, finding a language to confer materiality—in words, in actions, in visibilia—on the otherwise unseen. We come to know Herbert's Jesus and Whitman's future reader and Ashbery's Francesco as they were not known before they were cast as the invisible listeners hearkening to the poet's voice.

Notes

Introduction

1. Poem no. 13, *The Poetical Works of Gerard Manley Hopkins.* ed. Norman H. MacKenzie (Oxford: The Clarendon Press, 1990), 73.

2. Here, as elsewhere, I use the masculine pronoun for the poet and speaker, since my three examples are male. There are, of course, many women poets (e.g., Emily Brontë) who have addressed an invisible listener.

3. Certain critics have voiced attacks on the inevitable solitude of the lyric genre. Male sonneteers are said to have "silenced" the very woman they address by not giving her space to reply (though this accusation is never directed at the comparable practice of female sonneteers from Mary Wroth to Elizabeth Barrett Browning). The presumed poverty of social reference of the lyric has been criticized (with reference to Wallace Stevens) by the poet Mark Halliday, who then links Stevens to Ammons and Ashbery. Ashbery, he asserts, offers merely "release from meaning":

> I think that from the perspective of the year 2040, Ashbery will be a curiosity, an astonishingly copious curiosity, and smart people in 2040 will find it sweetly baffling that smart people in the 80s and 90s took Ashbery so seriously. His work is delicious, in small servings, as a release from meaning, giving us a playground where we feel, for awhile, that we can survive on only the whiffs of meaning. ["Walking and Talking: An Interview with Mark Halliday by Matthew Cooperman," in *The Writer's Chronicle* 34 (February 2002): 56–63, 61.]

4. Walt Whitman, "A Noiseless Patient Spider," "Till the gossamer thread you fling catch somewhere, O my soul."

5. Julia Kristeva, *Intimate Revolt: The Powers and Limits of Psychoanalysis,* 2 vols., tr. Jeanine Herman, (New York: Columbia University Press, 2002),

81

vol 2. "[S]uppose the imaginary offered the most immediate, most subtle, but also most dangerous access to the intimate. . . . The imaginary, neither real nor symbolic, appears in all its logic—and risk—when introduced through fantasy" (63). What Kristeva subsequently remarks about translation is equally true of the poet's attempts to formulate new possibilities of intimacy: the social qualities of present life are inevitably embedded in the work of formulating a new life.

> The object of a lucid yet passionate love, the new language is a pretext for rebirth: new identity, new hope. The translator aspires to assimilate it absolutely, while at the same time more or less unconsciously insufflating it with the archaic rhythms and instinctual bases of his native idiom. . . . Starting with this breach, the old as well as the new, the original family as well as the new community appear both endearing and problematic: an inconsolable questioning, the never-extinguished anxiety. (241)

6. The term is Yeats's, from "Upon a House shaken by the Land Agitation," in which he speaks of "gradual Time's last gift, a written speech / Wrought of high laughter, loveliness and ease."

Chapter One: George Herbert and God

1. Herbert's chief debt to the liturgy is to the Psalms, which employ such a range of tones in addressing God that Herbert could not but profit from their example. Yet they do not exhibit his winning intimacy with God as contemporary friend; and though a long study could be made of the relation of the Psalms to Herbert's poetry and prose, it is not, I think, relevant to my purposes here.

2. George Herbert, *Works*, ed. F. E. Hutchinson (Oxford: The Clarendon Press, 1964). All citations are from this edition, and are identified by page numbers in the text. I have silently modernized "then" to "than" when that meaning is intended.

3. "Memoriae Matris Sacrum III," in *The Latin Poetry of George Herbert*, tr. Mark McCloskey and Paul R. Murphy (Athens: Ohio University Press, 1965), 129–31:

Verùm heus, si nequeas caelo demittere matrem,
   Sítque omnis motūs nescia tanta quies,
Fac radios saltem ingemines, vt dextera tortos
   Implicet, & matrem, matre manente, petam.

The editors translate:

O yet if you my mother
Can't send down from heaven, if your
Huge immobility no motion knows,
Multiply your rays of light
That I may wind and twist
My hands in them, and, my mother staying
Where she is, climb up to her.

[*Latin Poetry*, 129–31]

4. See, in Herbert's *A Priest to the Temple*, chapter 16, *The Parson a Father* [*Works*, 250]:

The Countrey Parson is not only a father to his flock, but also professeth himselfe throughly of the opinion, carrying it about with him as fully, as if he had begot his whole Parish. And of this he makes great use. For by this means, when any sinns, he hateth him not as an officer, but pityes him as a Father: and . . . considers the offender as a child, and forgives.

5. The same metaphor of one clinging to a rock appears in one of the Latin elegies for Herbert's mother:

Nunc sorti pateo, expositus sine matre procellis,
Lubricus, & superans mobilitate salum.
Tu radix, tu petra mihi firmissima, Mater,
Ceu Polypus, chelis saxa prehendo tenax.

[*Latin Poetry*, 144–45]

The editors translate (rather unfortunately) as follows:

Now bare to chance, without a mother,
To storms defenseless, mercurial,
More fluid than the open sea, am I.

Root and staunchest rock you are to me, my mother;
I am as polyps, fixed by tentacles to rocks.

6. I pass over here the model of intimacy in which Jesus comes to the heart by way of the bread and wine of the Eucharist. Herbert's first version of this model can be seen in a poem found in the early Williams manuscript but not included in *The Temple*, "The H. Communion" [200–201]. Although it aims at intimacy of address at the beginning— "O Gratious Lord"—and at the end—"My God, give mee all Thee"—it departs from that intimacy during the rest of its course, when it is distracted from emotional response by an intellectualizing theology:

I could beleeue an Impanation
At the rate of an Incarnation,
        If thou hadst dyde for Bread. . . .

Into my soule this cannot pass;
fflesh (though exalted) keeps his grass
        And cannot turn to soule.
Bodyes & Minds are different Spheres,
Nor can they change their bounds & meres,
        But keep a constant Pole.

The Temple's "The H. Communion" [52–53], a later poem, takes on slightly greater intimacy ("[B]y the way of nourishment and strength, / Thou creep'st into my breast") without maintaining such closeness throughout the poem. Another Communion poem ("The Banquet" [181–82]) addresses the bread and wine, and speaks of God in the third person: "God, to show how farre his love / Could improve,/ Here, as broken, is presented." The tone is not intimate except in the initial address to the bread and wine ("Welcome sweet and sacred cheer, / Welcome deare"). It would seem that the species of bread and wine alone were not sufficiently "human" to stir Herbert to intimacy of presentation. It is only when the sacred banquet is translated to heaven, and given a personal host ("Love"), that Herbert writes the great and intimate poem "Love (III)."

7. Each closing line represents another variant on ethical failure. "I would not do that" reflects on will; "I could not do that" reflects on one's ego-ideal; "I cannot do that" reflects on one's actions; "Nor would I do that" denies a self-accusation of wrongdoing; and the last—"Yet use I not my foes, as I use thee"—presumes an ultimate baseness.

8. I cannot resist instancing a model of a different sort of intimacy— that between role and self, self and Christ—in the poem "Aaron." The poem does not use tones of intimacy; it is addressed by a priest first to himself and (at the end) to his congregation. But as the speaker puts off his sinful self (St. Paul's "old man") and assumes the role of priest (by donning the vestments of Aaron) he finds himself transfigured into a true Aaron and thus into Aaron's antitype, Christ. The ultimate indissolubility of liturgical role and redeemed private self is enacted by the way in which each of the five five-line stanzas repeats in identical order the same five rhyme-words ("head," "breast," "dead," "rest," and "drest"). The structure of five (lines) multiplied by five (stanzas) repeating five (talismanic) words is of course a symbol of perfection. I give the first and last stanzas. All stanzas allude to Aaron's miter and breastplate (the latter containing the Urim and the Thummim, Lights and Perfections) and to his robe ornamented at the hem with pomegranates and golden bells (Exod. 28):

> Holinesse on the head,
> Light and perfections on the breast,
> Harmonious bells below, raising the dead
> To leade them unto life and rest:
> Thus are true Aarons drest.

. . . .

> So holy in my head,
> Perfect and light in my deare breast,
> My doctrine tun'd by Christ, (who is not dead,
> But lives in me while I do rest)
> Come people; Aaron's drest.

[174]

85

As vestment becomes body, and body becomes the body of Christ, the priest is "with God" in a sense different from that enabled by writing verse or hearing a celestial echo or participating in a heavenly banquet. Becoming Christ ("Christ is my onely head, / My alone onely heart and breast"), the priest does not need to address Christ; in this experiment in intimacy-by-identity of role and subject, apostrophic intimacy is unnecessary.

9. I take it that in reading this poem aloud, one treats the word "Echo" as a silent stage direction. It is not meant to be uttered aloud, since to do so would be to destroy the aural echo-effect: "high? / I."

10. Cf. Wallace Stevens, "Tea at the Palaz of Hoon": "And there I found myself more truly and more strange"—a sentence applicable to the experience of both a poet in creating a poem and a person in an intimate friendship.

11. The primary Biblical source for "Love (III)" is Luke 13:37: "Blessed are those servants, whom the lord when he cometh shall find watching: verily I say unto you, that he shall gird himself, and make them to sit down to meat, and will come forth and serve them." Yet Herbert encompasses, in his figure of Love, the Father ("Who made the eyes but I?"), the sanctifying Holy Spirit ("You shall be he"), and the Son ("And know you not, sayes Love, who bore the blame?"). The figure of Love is conceived as existing beyond the implicit diminution intrinsic to gender of either kind, which cannot—since ascribed gender must be male or female—represent wholeness, let alone the three-persons-in-one of the Trinity evoked by the figure of Love.

12. See, in chapter 11 of *A Priest to the Temple*, Herbert's remarks on the ethical base of *The Parson's Courtesie* [*Works*, 243]:

> The Countrey Parson owing a debt of Charity to the poor, and of Courtesie to his other parishioners, he so distinguisheth, that he keeps his money for the poor, and his table for those that are above Alms. Not but that the poor are welcome also to his table, whom he sometimes purposely takes home with him, setting them close by him, and carving for them, both for his own humility, and their comfort, who are much cheered with such friendliness.

13. See Michael C. Schoenfeldt, *Prayer and Power: George Herbert and Renaissance Courtship* (Chicago: University of Chicago Press, 1991). Schoenfeldt sees "Love (III)" as a poem in which power relations are masked by courtesy:

> Deference and submission, normally expressions of one's willingness to adapt to the will of another, are exposed as vehicles for self-assertion and intransigence.... The impact of ["Love (III)"] derives from its rigorous investigation of the process by which the pendular rhythms of politeness mask the effectual operations of power. [205]

Schoenfeldt also offers a reading in which "Love (III)" punningly suggests an erotic subtext:

> The speaker's subsequent offer of service—"My deare, then I will serve"—plays, as does Herbert's sonnet to his mother, upon bawdy and devout senses of "service." In offering to serve, then, the speaker expresses his desire to preserve some vestige of social and sexual sufficiency. Love answers with a command that both dismisses and fulfills this desire—"You must sit down, sayes Love, and taste my meat." Oral dependency supplants genital potency as an expression of love and union. Unable to stand or serve—both euphemisms for maintaining an erection—the speaker must "sit and eat." [258]

Such readings "against the grain" of Herbert's presumed intent in the poem closing *The Temple* seem to me to undo the gentle comedy of Herbert's language and plot. To psychoanalyze a poet after the fact, suggesting that he is writing about the soul's entrance into heaven in terms of a power play and an erection, seems to me a dubious form of critical assistance.

14. The vexed liturgical question of whether the Christian should sit (as a guest at a Feast) or kneel (in humility) when receiving the Eucharist is discussed by Herbert in chapter 22 of *A Priest to the Temple* [*Works*, 259], where the poet offers the reason for each posture, and then says that posture matters less than Christian accord. "Contentiousnesse" rather than posture is cause for scandal:

For the manner of receiving, as the Parson useth all reverence himself, so he administers to none but to the reverent. The Feast indeed requires sitting, because it is a Feast; but man's unpreparednessse asks kneeling. Hee that comes to the Sacrament, hath the confidence of a Guest, and hee that kneels, confesseth himself an unworthy one, and therefore differs from other Feasters: but hee that sits, or lies, puts up to an Apostle: Contentiousnesse in a feast of Charity is more scandall than any posture.

Herbert's narrator in "Love (III)" shows the humility of one who senses his own unworthiness, but Love requires of him the posture of a guest at a Feast.

Chapter Two: Walt Whitman and the Reader-in-Futurity

1. All quotations are drawn from Walt Whitman, *Leaves of Grass and Other Writings*, ed. Michael Moon (New York: Norton Critical Edition, 2002) and will be cited by page number within the text. In the case of long poems, line numbers will be cited preceding the page number. When necessary, the date of the edition of *Leaves of Grass* in question will also be given. When I refer to the speaker of a poem as "Whitman" or "the poet," I mean, of course, the fictive person who is the protagonist of *Leaves of Grass*.

In the phrase "and the best liquor afterward" there is an implicitly blasphemous, or at least transvaluative, reference to the wedding feast at Cana, in which, after the supply of wine has been exhausted, the water transformed into wine by Jesus is pronounced the best wine of all.

2. The original reading may be found in Walt Whitman, *Leaves of Grass: Comprehensive Reader's Edition*, ed. Harold W. Blodgett and Sculley Bradley (New York: New York University Press, 1965) 136.

3. Whitman subsequently revised this line to include the address "Dear son," suggesting that of the two camerados, one is older and one younger. In the 1855 original, although the tone is perhaps that of an initiate to an "eleve," the familial epithet—distancing the comradeship from the erotic realm—is not present.

4. George Herbert, in "The H. Communion" (addressing God) says that He does not convey Himself to the poet "in rich furniture, or fine

aray," but "by the way of nourishment and strength / Thou creep'st into my breast" [*Works*, 52].

5. Cf. Herbert again, "Redemption," in which the soul searches for God: "In heaven at his manor I him sought; / . . . knowing his great birth / Sought him accordingly in great resorts; / In cities, theatres, gardens, parks, and courts." When the pilgrim finds his Lord in the midst of "a ragged noise and mirth / Of thieves and murderers," he is told, "Your suit is granted" [*Works*, 40]. Another such search, in "The Pilgrimage" [*Works*, 141–52], remains, as we have seen above, unrewarded.

6. This is the passage that Hopkins may have imitated, when, in "That Nature Is a Heraclitean Fire and of the comfort of the Resurrection," he described a tumultuous sky after a storm:

> Cloud-puffball, torn tufts, tossed pillows | flaunt forth, then
>   chevy on an air-
> built thoroughfare: heaven-roysterers, in gay-gangs | they
>   throng; they glitter in marches.
>
>   [*Poetical Works*, 197]

Chapter Three: John Ashbery and the Artist of the Past

1. John Ashbery, *Selected Poems* (New York: Viking, 1985) 178. Henceforth cited in the text as *SP*.

2. John Ashbery, *Reported Sightings* (New York: Knopf, 1989), 288. Henceforth cited in the text as *RS*.

3. "Out of Time," *New Yorker* (March 8, 2004), 84.

4. See also Ashbery's brief essay on Parmigianino, *RS*, 31–33.

Index

Index

Index